How & Why
Male Dominance
Plagues Humanity!

The Ultimate Challenge
for
Females!

How & Why Male Dominance Plagues Humanity!

The Ultimate Challenge For Females!

Boyé Lafayette De Mente

A PHOENIX BOOKS ORIGINAL

Phoenix Books / Publishers

ABOUT THE AUTHOR

Boyé Lafayette De Mente is an internationally known author of 50-plus pioneer books on the business practices, cultures and languages of China, Japan, Korea and Mexico, beginning with the classic *Japanese Etiquette & Ethics in Business* published in 1959 and still in print in its 7th edition at McGraw-Hill. He has also written extensively about the manners and morals of Americans. A list of his titles is included at the back of this book.

For a full listing and synopses of the author's
books see his websites: www.BoyeDeMente.com
and www.AuthorsOnlineBookshop.com
*All of his titles are available from the #1 online bookseller.

CONTENTS

PART I

Male Dominance

God-Based Morality

Profit as the New God

The Black Hole of Politics

The Entertainment Cesspool

The Advertising Conspiracy

The News Media Virus

Cultural Sabotage

Parental Failures & Fixes

Teacher Failures & Fixcs

Admin Failures & Fixes

PART II

Living in today's World

The Age of Robots!

Technology as God

Why Humanity Needs a
New Cultural Paradigm

Guidelines for a New
Cultural Paradigm

Learning Lessons from Japan's
Famous Samurai Class

The Extraordinary
Benefits of Modern-Day Karate

The Spirit, the Intellect &
the Distant Dream

The New Education Paradigm

INTRODUCTION

The problems afflicting the world at large are not simple or isolated. They are symptoms of the overall failure of cultures as a whole. These partial or complete cultural failures include all of the institutions and organizations that are associated with civilization—economic, educational, political, and social.

There are still some shining lights in American and other cultures but broadly speaking the various facets of the cultures are a mishmash of conflicting principles, faulty planning, incompetent execution and a number of cancerous elements that represent a serious threat to the world.

Where the United States is concerned the need for a different education model that would make it possible for Americans to achieve more of their intellectual, emotional and spiritual potential and actually live up to the American dream has been starkly obvious since the mid-1900s, and yet the problems are getting worse instead of better.

One of the most crucial reforms that must be made is the creation of a new economic order; something that became painfully obvious with the financial and subsequent business collapse that occurred in 2007—a collapse that was analyzed in a searing documentary film entitled *Inside Job* by Charles Ferguson, noted for his equally scathing *No End in Sight* review of the George W. Bush Administration's decision to invade Iraq.

In a revealing comment on the temper of the times Ferguson notes that the only person who went to jail for the disastrous *Inside Job* scam was Kristin Davis, a madam who provided prostitutes for Wall Street bankers. He accused the Obama White House-appointed finance industry executives with further enabling and enriching their Wall Street cronies while doing nothing for the people.

One of the more dangerous and frightening elements of American culture today is that most people born after 1950 know very little if anything about American history, or the history of humanity in general. For all of the brilliance, invention and innovation by individual Americans and small groups of people the overall intellectual capacity and knowledge of Americans in general is low. Even more of a problem is the fact that irrational attitudes and behavior commonly override not only common sense but any pretense of high moral values.

Where basic education is concerned the oddly entitled 2010 documentary *Waiting for 'Superman*, created by film director Davis Guggenheim, reviews the shortcomings of American education in a way that brings them home to the average person.

In essence, the film blames teachers' unions for resisting merit pay, teacher standards and changes in tenure for many of education's shortcomings, and politicians for "pouring money into a broken system" which does not result in fixing anything. [The odd title of the film was based on a comment by charter school proponent Geoffrey Canada who said that when he was a kid in a poor school he realized that there was no Superman, that no one was coming to save him or his fellow students.]

The undeniable point is that none of the education problems are going to be resolved without a fundamental revolution that addresses all of the major cultural failures that plague not only Americans but mankind in general, beginning with moral principles based on universal common sense rather than irrational religious dogma.

The creation and implementation of high moral standards has to start with secular education, with the necessary knowledge, values and goals instilled in the minds of the young—a herculean task that must be promoted and carried out by parents, teachers and others who recognize and understand the failures of present-day culture and will devote their careers and their lives to creating a new cultural paradigm. The first stage of this revolution has to be an understanding of the elements of the challenge, especially the role that money and politics play not only in education but in life across the board.

The Asian Example

On the education front most Americans are aware—or should be aware—that Chinese, Japanese, Korean and other Asian students commonly rank higher in their scholastic scores than Americans. The reason for this is simple.

Asian parents are obsessed with their children becoming educated, and program them both mentally and physically to study hard and excel in their classes. They know from several thousand years of history that their children cannot improve their economic or social well-being without an education.

In the mid-1950s Japan, for example, became famous—or notorious, depending on your viewpoint—for its *juku* [juu-kuu], so-called "Cram Schools" in English, which were privately run after-hours schools operated all over the country for students whose parents were determined that they would be able to get into the most prestigious high schools and universities—a university degree being absolutely essential for any white collar job, with the best jobs in industry going to the few thousands who graduated from Tokyo University or one of the other top two or three universities. To get into one of these top universities you had to have attended a top high school.

Hundreds of thousands of Japanese grammar and high school-age students went directly from their regular public schools to these private schools where they were required to study for up to four additional hours each weekday and often on Saturdays as well.

9

Even before the advent of Cram Schools, before World War II, many Japanese students were so diligent and determined that after memorizing every word on the page of an English dictionary, for example, they would eat the page!

There is still another form of private schools in Japan known as *Yobikō* [Yoh-be-kohh] that is aimed specifically at preparing students for high school and college entrance examinations.

While this extreme dedication to education in Japan diminished dramatically following the adoption of American attitudes and ways from around 1960 on, it still remains a potent force, especially among females.

Among Asian-Americans this dedication to the value of education has been passed on from one generation to the next, and continues today among families that have been in the United States since the 1800s.

It is still part of the American mindset of school-age children and some parents to celebrate when schools have to let out early or close entirely for whatever reason—a mentality that goes back to the time when schooling was not connected to making a living on a farm or in a factory. All that was required then was brawn, some physical skills and endurance.

Now there is more to be concerned about than competition from Asian-American students. Early in this century the Chinese, Indian and South Korean governments in particular mandated that the level and quality of education in their countries would be increased on a regular, unending basis, like the Japanese concept of *kaizen* [kigh-zen] meaning "continuous improvement"—which played a major role in tiny Japan becoming the second largest economy in the world in less than 20 years following the destruction it suffered during World War II.

The reason for the official continuous education improvement policy of these countries is that they mean to be on the winning side in the new global economy, and they know that a high standard of education is the key.

The programs Asian leaders have mandated include comprehensive and intensive studies in math and science *and in the languages and cultures of their international competitors.*

As was the case with Japan's Phoenix-like rise from the devastation of World War II to become the world's second largest economy between 1950 and 1970, neither the American business community nor politicians paid serious attention to the rise of China in a similar time-frame and for exactly the same reasons—free access to the consumer-driven American market, out-sourcing by American companies and the American government (military supplies in particular during the Korean and Vietnam wars) and a flood of American technology.

The overall failure of the American education system bears responsibility for this head-in-the-mud myopia.

A total reformation of the education model is, in fact, the most critical problem facing all of mankind today—education that is rational and comprehensive; education that provides the information and skills that are essential for people to overcome their ignorance and willful stupidity and achieve their fullest possible potential.

There is ample knowledge about *why* these problems exist and what their solutions are. In addition to documentation provided by thousands of would-be reformers in lectures, in articles and in books, dozens of thousands of pages of detailed accounts of all of the problems afflicting public education as well as common sense solutions to the problems are available on the Internet.

Sociologist Nathan Glazer listed the following five elements by which one could predict the success or failure of elementary students and schools: the number of days students are absent from school; the number of hours students spend watching television at home; the number of pages

11

students read for home-work; the quality and quantity of reading material in the homes of students; and whether or not there are two parents in the home.

These factors—as profound and as far-reaching as they are—do not begin to suggest the variety and volume of cultural time-bombs that are ticking away in the United States and are impervious to half-hearted attempts to defuse them.

In the early 1980s efforts began in the United States to remedy the worst of the practices in education, but despite these attempts most of the more vital issues were still unresolved at the end of the first decade of the 21st century—primarily because of the underlying cultural irrationalities and ignorance that have been characteristic of societies since the advent of civilizations.

Well over half of all Americans regard the current state of education in the U.S. as a quagmire and are clamoring for fixes. The solutions they most often propose: pay teachers more so smarter people will become teachers; merit pay for teachers based on their effectiveness; using standardized test scores to measure teacher-performance; more involvement by parents; end the tenure system; better teacher training; monitoring by more experienced teachers—all common sense ideas that range from difficult to impossible to implement because the system is not self-correcting.

The whole approach to education should be brought up to date by optimizing new knowledge and new technologies, and kept flexible enough that it can evolve with the times. To arrive at this new approach will require an unprecedented educational process that will put the majority of people on the same page so they can agree on and implement the changes that must take place.

This will require the reprogramming of the mindset of a vast number of Americans who are steeped in political and religious dogma.

The Incredible Cultural Failures

The specific reasons for the failure of virtually every aspect of American culture include gender differences and male-oriented and male-directed moralities.

The argument could be made that the weaknesses of the American public education system gave birth to all of the other cultural failures, but that is a shortsighted and false view. When available public education has always taken a back seat to religions and politics and until recent times was not available to most people—especially to females—*because* of religious and political opposition.

The single most important factor in the overall failure of human cultures has, in fact, been male dominance. The second most important factor has been the influence of male-dominated religions, including Judaism, Christianity and Islam, all of which embody the worst characteristics of cults—a cult, by definition, being a system of community or religious worship and ritual, especially one focusing upon a single deity or spirit; an obsessive devotion or veneration for a person, principle or ideal; an exclusive group of people sharing an esoteric interest.

Boyé Lafayette De Mente

14

MALE DOMINANCE

The Male Sex Thing

Virtual and real male dominance over females in virtually every group of human beings that has ever existed has resulted in ignorance, willful stupidity, cruelty and violence plaguing mankind since day one.

As noted in my book *THE ORIGINS OF HUMAN VIOLENCE! - Male Dominance, Ignorance, Religions & Self-Willed Stupidity!,* male discrimination against females did not begin as a religious thing. It evolved naturally from the genetic programming of males, so when men created gods their gods naturally consigned women to an inferior status.

It goes without saying that males in virtually all species of life are genetically designed to be sexually aggressive, to impregnate as many females as possible and to take by force and keep exclusive sexual rights to as many females as possible.

This instinctive behavior of human males was buttressed by their recognition that *females are inherently more sexually potent than males,* and it was this sexual reality that resulted in early males doing everything in their power—physically, emotionally, intellectually and spiritually—to control women, to make them subservient not only sexually but in all other aspects of life.

To again paraphrase from the above book, the emergence of civilizations put a kink in the sexual monopoly of big strong males. After the advent of larger organized societies most men, officially at least, had to limit themselves to just one mate at a time, but in most societies many males made sure they still had access to mistresses, concubines, harems and prostitutes.

Then in what is now referred to as the Western world—as opposed to Asia—along came Judaism, Christianity and Islam—all of which were created and controlled by men and all of which established "god-given" laws controlling the sexual behavior of men and women, with the laws naturally skewered in favor of men. In these male-created and controlled religions, females were an after-thought created to serve men.

As time went by, overly zealous religious leaders and theologians—all males and often men who feared women—began to preach that women were naturally evil and would seduce and debase men if they had the slightest opportunity. They then created a world in which women had to deny and suppress their own sexuality, resulting in indescribable frustration and suffering to the point that mental and physical ailments among women became common.

What all of the ancient world's alpha males and all of the religious clerics, ministers, popes, priests, shamans—or whatever they are called—misunderstood or ignored was the fundamental sexual nature of human beings.

Those misguided and id/gonad-driven males denied or ignored the fact that among all members of the animal kingdom, including human beings, sexuality comes right after survival in the built-in gene-powered drives. Furthermore, unlike some of their lower-order relatives male humans are "in heat" all the time. Females, on the other hand, want sex only on certain occasions and with selected males.

Of course, there were enough valid social and political reasons for male leaders of early societies and religions to curb the sexual behavior of men and women. But the way they went about it was both inhuman and cruel. First of all, they put most of the responsibility on women, accusing them of not being able to control their sexual nature and therefore being a clear and present danger to society.

Throughout the history of Jewish, Christian, Islamic and other male-controlled societies virtually all women have been forced to suppress their natural sexuality to a degree which, as mentioned earlier, left them frustrated and subject to a variety of physical and mental ailments.

Remarkably, more than 2,000 years ago Hippocrates came up with the word "hysteria" to describe these ailments but he didn't understand that they were caused by pent-up unused sexual energy.

Just as remarkable—given the ongoing ignorance of males and the influence of religions—in the 1880s an American doctor came up with the idea of using an electric vibrator as a medical treatment for women suffering from "female hysteria"—having somehow discovered that when the genitals of women suffering from "hysteria" were stimulated the symptoms of the malady disappeared.

Even after the doctors discovered that orgasms eliminated this ancient "disease" neither they nor their patients realized that the cathartic release following genital stimulation had anything whatsoever to do with lack of sufficient sexual activity. They called it "paroxysm."

Despite the "sexual emancipation" of women that began in the United States in the early 20th century, picked up speed in the 1950s, and now often appears to be moving at the speed of light, most American women still today are constrained in their sexual behavior, repressing, ignoring or denying their sexuality to a significant degree.

With the "power of God" in their hands, male religious leaders long ago succeeded in brain-washing most women to not only accept the sexual restrictions placed on their behavior, but to also become firm believers in the righteousness of the laws—written and unwritten—that controlled their lives.

As said, this male position did not originally derive from any divine source. It was nothing more than a way for men to control the sexual behavior of all females in their group or tribe. Because males were controlled by their animalistic instincts they did not want other males to have sexual access to the females around them—and like lower animals they were driven to mate with as many females as possible in an instinctive urge to have off-spring.

Subsequent religious taboos, customs and laws designed to control and limit the sexual behavior of both males and females were to have incredible unintentional results.

Traditionally, the only people who were exempt from these restrictions—or simply chose to ignore them—were the men in charge. Both lay and religious leaders have historically broken the laws they enacted and required common people to obey.

One of the more recent examples of this syndrome was the scandal that hit the Catholic Church at the end of the 20th century when rampant sexual activity by homosexual and pedophile priests was revealed—a practice that had been going on from day one but was kept quiet by Church leaders as well as condoned by those in these categories who had risen to high positions in the Church.

Because of this scandal new fuel was added to the growing lay and some priestly opposition to the Catholic Church doctrine of requiring priests to remain celibate.

The idea that abstaining from sexual intercourse with members of the opposite sex results in males and females remaining pure and saintly, goes back several thousand years. But it was not until the 4th century A.D. that it first cropped up in the so-called Western Church. And it was not until the mid-11th century that Pope Gregory VII issued a decree forbidding priests from marrying.

The decree prohibiting priests from marrying or engaging in sex with females was reaffirmed by Popes in the

12th century and again in the 16th century. Despite growing opposition to this ancient practice the decree was again reaffirmed in 2010 by Pope Benedict XVI.

The idea that celibacy contributes to purity in both a physical and divine sense is, of course, absolute nonsense. What it does do is subject the individual to enormous stress that manifests itself in a variety of ways that have long been obvious but have been ignored by religious leaders.

One of these ways appears to be what the news media refers to as "sex-addiction" among a growing number of males. In 2010 *Los Angeles Times* writer Harriet Ryan did a lengthy piece on a dramatic increase in the number of therapists who specialize in male sex-addiction cases. The column was prompted by a storm of publicity about the sexual affairs of several prominent male celebrities— which in itself was not new because movie actors as well as sports celebrities have long been noted as much for their sexual activities as for their professional performances.

Not surprisingly, the news media brought a number of psychiatrists into the fray who said there was no proof that a man or a woman could become addicted to sex and suffer withdrawal symptoms if deprived of sex the way drug addicts do. In any event, the male sex-addiction story was like raw meat to scandal tabloids as well as mainstream news media.

And if that was not enough to once again reveal the public role that sex now plays in life, *The Arizona Republic* newspaper ran the original *Los Angeles Times story* next to a large medical institute advertisement that featured the naked legs of a woman lying on her back in an obvious sex position.

This kind of sleaze news and advertising is more fall-out from the religious dogma that sex not intended for procreation is a sin, but it is a minor blip compared to other damage caused by religious doctrines.

One of the most irrational and inhuman policies of the Catholic Church has been its prohibition of any form of artificial contraception, labeling it a grave sin against the will of God. But finally, in an interview with a German journalist in 2010, Pope Benedict made the following deliberately convoluted comment: "There may be a basis in the case of some individuals, as perhaps when a male prostitute uses a condom, where this can be a first step in the direction of a moralization, a first assumption of responsibility."

This comment appears in a book entitled *Light of the World: The Pope, the Church and the Signs of the Times,* by Peter Seewald, released in November 2010. The Pope made the above comment when the journalist asked him if it wasn't "madness" for the Vatican to forbid a high-risk population from using condoms.

The Pope added that the Vatican does not regard the use of condoms by male prostitutes as a real or moral solution, and followed this with a weak-kneed comment that "it might be a first step in a movement toward a different way, a more human way, of living sexuality."

When asked about the Pope's unprecedented comments Catholic religious authorities said it was obviously a change in the ideology of the Vatican...a situation that once again exposed the irrationality and inhumanity of the traditional teachings of the Catholic Church.

What will help drive the Catholic Church to change its ways or disappear into the dustbins of history is the fact that by the year 2010 over 100,000 priests had left the Church in order to get married.

One of these was Alberto Cutie, a former poster boy for the Catholic Church and a popular radio and television talk show host who fell in love with a woman and left the Church in order to marry her. He had previously written a book, *Real Life, Real Love,* which got him into a lot of trouble with Catholic leaders because in the book he expressed his disappointment with the inhuman policies of the Church.

In a second book, *DILEMMA: A Priest's Struggle with Faith and Love*, published in January 2011, Cutie went further in his criticism of the hidebound policies of the Vatican, saying what a great many other priests would surely like to say. He is now a happily married father and a priest in an Episcopal church in Florida.

The Primitive Male Mind

The gene-based need for males to dominate on all areas of human endeavor resulted in selfish interests, tribalism, territorialism and discrimination against race, skin color and other religious beliefs becoming male characteristics.

In many males these elements, separately or combined, override logic, objectivity and rationality in both subtle and obvious ways, resulting in behavior that is negative instead of positive, disruptive instead of harmonizing and destructive instead of constructive.

Examples of irrational, illogical and harmful behavior are so deeply ingrained in the minds of many males that they have become institutionalized and ritualized in customs and laws and have persisted since the dawn of human history...because the essential mindset of males has not changed and people with invested interests in the customs and laws have made sure that they continue to survive.

Humanity will continue to be plagued by ignorance, stupidity and violence as long as religious doctrines continue to preach and enforce the superiority of men and the inferiority of women, and prevent women from bringing their innate sense of compassion, cooperation and goodwill to the world at large.

Obviously, the sexual nature of males and the sex-based arrogance that led them to automatically assume that they were superior to females was to have results that went far beyond the oppression of females.

This arrogance and the cultural systems it created continue to plague mankind, and despite the examples of women who have ascended to power in the business and political worlds the underlying faults and failures of the religious-empowered syndrome remains in control in most societies.

An Incredible Phenomenon!

Wise men and women have known for millennia that it is immoral and inhuman to treat women as the property of males, but it was not until the 19th century that females began to make their voices heard—and often went to jail for it.

It is absolutely incredible that male-created and dominated religious dogma prevented American women from having the right to vote until August 26, 1920, and still today many women around the world have far fewer political and social rights than men...all because of the hold that chauvinistic religions still have on the minds of people.

Women with few rights or virtually no rights at all have traditionally been brainwashed to accept the superiority of males and to be the most diligent followers of the very religions that have made them inferior creatures since day one.

But imagine what would happen if the vast majority of female Catholics, Christians, Jews and Muslims simply stopped going to and supporting the male-run churches and synagogues. Without female support, most of these institutions could not survive.

The End of a Long Dark Age

Throughout recorded history there have been instances of women making major contributions to the cultures of ancient societies, including Chinese, Greek, Hindu and Persian. But these contributions virtually stopped with the ascendancy of the Christian religion and its large off-shoots, particularly Islam, which taught that females were inferior to males and morally fit only for child-bearing and serving men.

The rapid growth of Christianity between 33-93 A.D., Islam from around 650 A.D., and the orthodox Catholic version of Christianity from 1054 A.D.—much of it by force of arms—resulted in an educational Dark Age for most of the world's males until around the end of the 19th century and for most of the world's females until the middle of the 20th century.

For century after century all education was controlled by religions that preached and followed the doctrine that females are inferior to males and must be kept in their place, which included keeping them ignorant and submissive—a policy that still today is followed by a number of religions.

It was not until the early years of the 20th century that it became acceptable and possible for large numbers of American and European females to attend elementary level schools, and it was to be several more decades before female enrollment in colleges grew into significant numbers.

The emergence of females as the equals of males in the workplace [outside of farms] began in earnest in the United States during World War II in the mid-20th century, when factories and offices had no choice but to hire several million women to replace the men engaged in a male-made war.

This phenomenon alone did more than anything else to release most of the chauvinist-inspired and religious-enforced bonds that had kept American and European women down and submissive throughout history.

By the 1970s the number of American women in college, in managerial positions in industry and in politics had increased to the point that they were making their influence felt.

This number has continued to increase, and in some professions—health, for example—there are as many females as males, and in a few professional areas females outnumber males. U.S. medical schools are now graduating more female doctors than male doctors.

By the end of the first decade of the 21st century women in industry had reached the point that they were having a profound influence on management philosophy and practices, introducing policies that were gender neutral and took into account the special role that females play in keeping the species alive by having and nurturing babies.

However, the three areas that remained barely touched by female influence were religions, politics and education, all of which have been bastions of male power since the origin of these institutions.

Despite the fact that new technology combined with other changes in American culture—good and bad—have given females far more opportunities and power than they have ever had since the origin of the species, their unique female mindset—so different from the male mind—has just begun to bring about fundamental changes in the institutions and enterprises that control American life.

It is, in fact, remarkable that the more outgoing and aggressive American females become the *more feminine American males become*—but the meeting of the two genders in a rational and positive compromise is still far away.

Ultimately, the genetic factor that nails the superiority of the female sex is that when women are free to think and behave in a way that is natural for them they are intrinsically more practical, more logical, more rational, and

24

more humane than males—all factors that are essential parts of the make-up of females because they are responsible for the actual creation and nurturing of human life.

If you make up a list of all of the cruel, destructive, evil, inhumane, savage and stupid things that have happened to human beings—and are, of course, still happening today— at least 99 percent of the people responsible for these things have been and are males.

The world desperately needs a new universal cultural paradigm that is devoid of theological-based myths and ignorance, and is based instead on the positive potential of the human species—a potential that now includes actually becoming god-like in the ability to do good...or evil.

GOD-BASED MORALITY

The Failure of Cult Religions

One of the original fundamental flaws in God-based Judaism, Christianity and Islam religions was divorcing the mind from the physical body; completely separating the needs of the body from the aspirations for a divine spiritual existence and eternal life...a concept that brought some comfort to ignorant humanity but the suffering it has caused is immeasurable.

It is, of course, an obvious and indisputable fact that man-made religious moralities have not succeeded in creating peace and goodwill among human beings. Every form of violence and ill-will imaginable is as common today, if not more so, than at any time in the history of the species.

The daily news is rife with references to God that are so irrational they go beyond being ridiculous. Clerics, preachers, terrorists, politicians, military men and others are constantly calling on God to bless them and their countries, and to bring death and destruction to their enemies.

There are far more damaging mental and moral aberrations across the board in societies where the guidelines for human behavior are based on an irrational male-oriented theological concept, with so-called entertainment being one of the most conspicuous examples.

It is incredible that modern-day entertainment—one of the biggest and most culturally influential of all industries—is more often than not based on catering to the most primitive, savage and gross side of humanity. The Christian Church in particular cannot compete with this form of mass cultural conditioning.

27

In fact, the Bill of Rights attached to the American Constitution forbids both the government and religious institutions from interfering with the public expression of the most gross and dehumanizing elements of "freedom of speech."

This black hole of immorality has come about in part because over the decades the laws of the United States have been skewered by ideologue politicians and other politicians under pressure from business leaders and others to favor and permit the debasement of humanity for the sake of profit—and most people at large accept this situation for a variety of reasons: they tell themselves they can't change it; that it is not their responsibility, and so on. It is also no doubt true that many people who publicly oppose this pandemic of profit-oriented cultural sleaze are strongly attracted to it.

The goal in producing and marketing sleaze is, of course, to make a profit. And the reason it is so profitable is because the attempts of religions and secular societies to control human behavior, despite their good intentions, have created a hunger for sleaze in all of its forms...especially those that are sex-related. Feeding this obsession drives the behavior of a large percentage of humanity.

Over the millennia many wise men and women have tried to replace religions with a philosophy of life that does not depend upon male-created gods but on simple common-sense universal rules and guidelines based on what is good and best for all humans. But just as obviously these attempts have failed because the intellect of human beings has not yet evolved to the point that people can transcend the religious moralities of the cultures they are raised in—or on their own overcome their built-in tendencies to think and behave in irrational and destructive ways.

It goes without saying that children are not capable of preventing themselves from being programmed like robots by their environment. To varying degrees they learn and accept the ways of their parents and other adults in their society—or they face a variety of punishments that range from being criticized, shamed and ostracized to—in some countries—being mutilated or murdered by their own fathers, brothers or other male adults.

Religions have, in fact, been and continue to be the source of much of the immorality and violence that has plagued humanity since their inception. You might say that after men created Gods in their own image everything went to Hell!

It is true, of course, that Judaism, Christianity and Islam were founded with the best of intentions but it was not long before they were turned into instruments of discrimination, oppression, violence and murder. Throughout their history mayhem and war have been among their primary legacies to mankind.

Over the millennia the vast majority of people who have accepted and attempted to live by the precepts of man-made religions—in other words, to live morally upright lives according to the precepts of their particular religion—have been the least powerful, the most downtrodden and the most victimized by the state and by the church…in other words, women.

In societies with god-based religions the word God itself has been turned into a catchall term that is used to justify murder by individuals and mass-killing by states. Pathological killers as well as the most upright members of societies beseech God to aid them in the destruction of their competitors and enemies, and praise God when they succeed.

That this incongruity is ignored by many of those who profess to believe in and follow the precepts of a "loving God" is pathological to the extreme. To be more precise, it is a form of cultural insanity. In virtually the same breath "God the Creator and Savior" becomes "God the Avenger, the Destroyer and the Bringer of Death" to one's enemies and disbelievers.

In human history good and bad have never existed in reality as fixed polar opposites. They have always been circumstantial and were whatever was prescribed at the time by the ruling powers—the clergy, the government and the military, or whichever one of these entities was dominant. These three institutions have also traditionally worked hand-in-hand to indoctrinate, subjugate and control people for their own purposes.

It goes without saying that for the vast majority of people survival and some degree of security and comfort take precedence over all other things. And if professing to believe in something like Islam, for example, will provide this security and comfort, even to a small degree, people programmed in that faith will believe and obey even the most irrational and inhuman dogma.

When the United States was founded some of the teachings of Christianity that are humane, positive and nurturing were incorporated into the laws of the land. But institutionalized Christianity was not made a state religion because it was clearly seen as an enemy of intellectual and personal freedom.

Why God-Based Religions Have Failed!

People in God-oriented societies commonly behave in ways that are contrary to religious teachings—in many cases because the teachings range from being impractical to inhuman, dangerous or worse, and following them makes no sense.

The concept that the "Kingdom of Heaven" is *within* the individual—not in some after-death place high in the sky—is probably the most important of all of the insights attributed to the historical Jesus, but it has been downplayed or ignored by all levels of God-based religions. In fact, according to the teachings of Christianity you can "sin" left and right and still go to Heaven if you confess and accept Jesus Christ [God manifested in the flesh to save mankind!], as your savior before you die—an incredible cop-out devised by religious leaders in an effort to make god-based religion more relevant to the masses.

Judaism, Christianity and Islam have never had all of the right answers for the spiritual needs of humanity—as history has so graphically demonstrated. Now, more and more so-called Christians are creating their own personal paths to fulfilling their spiritual needs.

And then, of course, some two-thirds of the world's population is *not* Christian or Jew—even if in name only. These are the Muslims, the Buddhists, the Hindus, and so on—most of whom have had good reason for disliking and fearing Christianity because of its intolerant claim of exclusivity and historical use of violence...not to mention the primitive, irrational elements of its theology.

India-American physician, author and public speaker Dr. Deepak Chopra has presented the most succinct explanation of the difference between religion and spirituality that I have ever heard or read. He reminds people that religions develop long after the occurrence of spiritual experiences. He notes that Jesus Christ was not a Christian and Buddha was not a Buddhist. "Those religious were ultimately constructed around an ideology, and of necessity took on the rigidity and risk of being taken over by people who were more interested in power-mongering and corruption. Spirituality, on the other hand, is a realm of awareness that is universal and goes beyond dogma."

Spirituality does indeed have a vital role to play in human life, but it has not been accurately or well presented by Judaism, Christianity or Islam—all of which were created by ignorant men who were beset by sexism, tribalism and racism that adversely affected their efforts to control human behavior.

In more ways than one, the God-based moralities of Judaism, Christianity and Islam have become an unfunny joke. The daily news is rife with references to God that are so irrational they go beyond being ridiculous.

Interestingly, Dennis Prager, the Jewish-American author and commentator on personal and social issues from morality to religion, says that most present-day Israelis are not religious in their day-to-day behavior. That is also true, of course, of most Americans, most of whom are too busy living.

Still, Americans are unique in the world. We make up the largest racially and culturally mongrelized group of people on the planet, and come closer than any other people to being color-blind, race-blind and religion-blind. For the most part people arriving from abroad [legally!] are viewed simply as people and for the most part have the same options and opportunities as prior arrivals and the native-born—and that is the power and the attraction of America.

The Anti-Female Religions

One of the most incredible continuing failings of the Catholic version of Christianity is the Vatican's position on women in the Church. Near the end of the 20th century a number of groups of Catholics who had distanced themselves from the rigid orthodoxy of the Vatican began to give women roles that had previously been the absolute preserves of males.

Some of these steps involved ordaining women as priests, a move that drew quick condemnation from the Vatican. In 2010 when break-away Catholic Churches ordained a number of female priests the move resulted in the Vatican condemning the action *as a grave sin on a par with the sexual abuse of children.* Incredible!

A spokesperson for the Vatican explained the position of the Church as following the precedent set by Jesus

Christ who, the spokesperson said, remained celibate all his life and ordained only males who had been baptized into the priesthood.

The bishop in charge later excommunicated a male priest who was involved in ordaining a female as a priest. The bishop explained his action by saying: *"Actions such as these are extremely serious and carry with them profoundly harmful consequences for the salvation of souls participating in this attempted ordination."*

That was an incredibly stupid, anti-human, anti-female thing for a high-ranking member of the Catholic Church to say, and it obviously represented the official position of the Church.

To permanently condemn one-half of humanity as inferior to males and not worthy of acting on behalf of the Church to teach moral behavior is an astounding example of the primitive mindset of both the male founders and present-day leaders of the Catholic Church—not to mention Islam, which is even more anti-female.

The chauvinistic and anti-human practices of the male-dominated Catholic and Islamic Churches have, of course, been the rule since day one and until modern times the power of the Church was such that women did not dare to question it. But until the power of the Church to defy common sense and to ignore the humanity it professes to hold sacred is broken it will continue to discriminate against women.

Why the Catholic Church has been able to maintain its power for such a long time is not a secret. Most males in the most "Catholic countries" have simply ignored the dogma and dictates of the Church in their normal "weekday" behavior—that has included cheating, lying, engaging in promiscuous sexual behavior and various forms and degrees of violence, most often against women.

As one honest Filipino Catholic priest once noted, "There is Catholic morality and there is Reality. Except when they go to Church on Sundays most Catholic laymen live in the world of Reality."

Until the fundamental errors that are built into the foundations of the largest and most powerful religions are acknowledged and corrected by their male rulers they will continue to be a major part of the failure of human beings to achieve even a small portion of their potential.

But given the pathological mentality of the Christian and Islamic Church lords this reformation will not happen until the religions are on the verge of becoming totally obsolete simply because the people at large will stop blindly supporting them.

Now that religions are no longer able to oppress people with impunity the gradual weakening of their hold on the mindset of well over half of humanity is, in fact, inevitably. Their "sins" are quickly made public. During this writing documented evidence along with testimony by members of the Catholic Church itself revealed that former Cardinal Joseph Ratzinger, elected Pope Benedict XVI in 2005, was fully aware of the abuse of young boys by pedophile priests going back to the 1980s but did nothing to stop it—finally resulting in media-driven investigations into his role in the cover-up.

After another Church scandal erupted in 2010 that further muddied the murky Catholic waters, Pope Benedict, to his credit, ordered a full-scale investigation of a Catholic group known as Regnum Christi operating in several countries when he finally became aware that its female members were treated like virtual slaves, forbidden to speak or make any decision on their own.

This followed an earlier "embarrassment" involving a secretive order known as the Legionaries of Christ, said to have been championed by Pope John Paul II, Pope Benedict's predecessor, whose founder sexually abused female members and fathered three children. During the investigation of the Legionaries founder the widespread abuse of women making up the ranks of Regnum Christi came to light and made news worldwide.

More and more people are becoming aware that the salvation of humanity lies in rational, factual education; not in male-created and male-dominated religious cults— and again if you question my referring to Judaism, Christianity and Islam as cults look up the word cult in your dictionary.

To give the Catholic Church its due it has played a major role in the healthcare industry by establishing and operating hospitals all over the world, and it was an early leader in establishing and operating schools that taught secular as well as spiritual subjects.

The Willful Stupidity Element!

One should be able to assume that present-day leaders of most religions are neither stupid nor ignorant. Even though most of them have been raised within the confines, restraints and taboos of their particular church and have been programmed by their environment and professional studies to accept the teachings of their particular religion, it requires a great deal of willful stupidity for them to deny what they see and hear in the real world, and in what their intrinsic common sense tells them.

While some of the motives of many of the clergy in all religions are pure and positive, continuing to pursue beliefs and practices that are patently false, invalid and anti-human requires a twisted mind. That is willful stupidity taken to the extreme.

Just a few days ago the news media carried interviews with two life-long religious pastors who admitted that they no longer believed in the existence of God—or any god for that matter. And how did they say they came to this startling insight? They said they did so by actually reading the Bible and discovering that it is primarily based on stories written by men totally ignorant of the nature, scope and grandeur of the cosmos attempting to prove there is a god who can and does break every law of nature but never actually does anything at all to save mankind from itself.

In simple terms, religious clergy have been brainwashed by their teachers and mentors and their overall environment—or they dupe themselves for some ulterior reason. Or they are perfectly aware of the duplicity of their position and actions and continue for reasons that have nothing to do with "saving souls."

Most of the world's religions have traditionally depended upon one thing to keep their uneducated members coming back for more. Fear! Fear that they will be condemned to Hell if they don't profess to believe and go through the prescribed rituals; and fear of the reprisals their Church and fellow members will take against them in this life if they don't conform to the prescribed behavior.

In earlier times reprisals by the Catholic Church ranged from being ostracized and shamed to being tortured and killed, often in the most horrible ways imaginable. In modern times the Church has moderated its punishment to social sanctions and the threat of eternal Hell instead of some form of execution.

Of course, the vast majority of Muslims are as non-violent and as tolerant as the average Christians and Jews but radical Islamic clerics remain hung up on the primitive beliefs and customs that were common when Islam was founded in the 7th century A.D.

Teaching children that they are going to burn in Hell forever if they don't obey the dictates of any religion is pathological, and so far from the original intent of religions that it is criminal. Prevailing upon young men and women to strap bombs to their bodies to seek out and kill as many people as possible in a struggle for religious and political power goes beyond pathology.

When the mothers of these brainwashed assassins say on camera how proud they are of their martyred sons and daughters it is unreal. It is even more unreal when it is discovered that the terrorists paid the families of the assassins. Only rational, non-religious education can cure this inhuman insanity.

The Life is Sacred Nonsense!

Another example of the nonsensical and dangerous influences of the combination of the male mind and religion is the concept that life is sacred. People in cultures that have been profoundly influenced by the Judeo-Christian God concept have been taught that life is sacred, and that only God can legitimately give and take life—human life, that is, since God (it is said) gave mankind dominion over all other life forms (otherwise we would not be able to kill and eat animals, fish, fowls and a variety of other forms of life without committing a sin).

The idea that a living god created all life—especially human life—and that life is sacred is so transparently invalid that it should have made any continuing belief in the concept patently impossible. And yet it is still one of the primary teachings of Judaism, Christianity and Islam.

The life-is-sacred myth is, of course, a concept created by the founders of Judaism and Christianity in an attempt to wean males away from their instincts to mistreat and kill others and to reprogram them to be respectful, kind and cooperative. In the eyes of these ancient founders only a god would be capable of such a miracle, and rightly so.

However, the primitive destructive instincts of human males were so strong that just being told that life was sacred was not enough to suppress these instincts in many men, with the result that mayhem and murder continued to be a distinguishing characteristic of humanity.

In fact, not long after the creation of the life-is-sacred concept, religious leaders themselves began to use violence in the name of their God in an attempt to force others to believe as they did and to obey the rules they had devised in an effort to control all thinking and behavior.

Incredibly, according to the Bible when Moses came down from Mt. Sinai with the first 10 Commandments and found that large numbers of his followers had created and were worshipping a golden calf and having a hell of a good time, he was so incensed that he smashed the stone tablet bearing the commandments and ordered his faithful followers to kill those who had stayed from the path. In one of the worst massacres in history his followers slaughtered over 3,000 fellow Jews—men, women and children. Moses then went back up on Mt. Sinai and [it is said] had God use his finger to rewrite the 10 Commandments on another stone slab!

Life is indeed precious to most human beings, but the history of humanity demonstrates that there is absolutely nothing sacred about it. Those who continue to profess belief in the sacred concept merely demonstrate that the human mind can be manipulated like any computer software program, and when confronted with reality they resort to claiming it is a matter of faith, not facts or reality.

It is the cosmos itself that is the Great Creator. It is infused with an inherent force to create life in forms and functions that are seemingly countless...in environments that are incredibly diverse and extreme. On Earth, new forms of life are discovered almost daily as scientists and others probe deeper into the oceans, into the subterranean depths of the Earth, and into isolated places on the surface of the Earth. [One of these days we will discover that life in varying forms is common among the billions of planets circling hundreds of billions of stars.]

Regardless of the form and function of any life form, in whatever environment, life to that particular form is precious, but, again, it is not sacred. All life forms, including humans, are subject to being obliterated, often in an instant, by other life forms and by nature.

Life is, in fact, based on life forms killing and eating other life forms—a food chain that is exactly the opposite of the religious concept that life is sacred. Nature creates life and life destroys life in order to survive and grow and become more adept at devouring other forms of life (not counting incidents of human cannibalism, of course).

The religious concept that is life is sacred crops up in virtually all areas of human life, and is routinely ignored by the majority. Opponents of abortions use the life-is-sacred argument to proclaim that abortions are a sin against God. This argument is also used by people who oppose the use of human stem cells in medical research.

Going one step farther, this rationale would apply to female eggs [most of which are disposed of naturally] and male sperm, most of which goes to "waste." In fact, there is an injunction in the Bible that describes masturbation as a grave sin, and states that "It is better to leave your seed in the belly of a whore than to cast it to the wind." How's that for a pithy summation of religious morality!

As stated, virtually all organic life forms on Earth exist by killing and eating other life forms—or in many cases eating them while they are *still alive*—in which case they are commonly promoted in some cultures as special treats. Now, only humans are normally not on the food chain... but don't turn your back on an alligator or any other really big lizard!

The Abortion Controversy!

An abortion is, of course, a dangerous and ignoble thing for a woman to go through, but done early enough and safely enough it is often a better choice than to have an unplanned, unwanted child. Being forced to have an unplanned and unwanted child—especially one that cannot be properly cared for and educated—because of an ancient and primitive religious belief is simply not right.

People who oppose abortions should spend their time and energy in helping women avoid unwanted pregnancies in the first place. There are millions of women around the world who are in desperate need of such help and every year they produce millions more children, many of whose lives are short and wretched.

As contradictory as it often is, human beings are the most advanced form of life known and some humans are capable of creating masterpieces of art, architecture, literature, music and technological marvels. In many areas, scientists and technicians are literally transforming life itself in "god-like" ways. And yet, large numbers of human beings are still driven by the instincts of their primitive ids to use force, to repress, to maim and murder to get what they want. This destructive behavior, on an individual as well as on group and national levels, is often done in the name of their God.

There is obviously a great deal of good in cultures influenced by Judaism, Christianity and Islam, but the myths and myopia these religions spawn and the irrational behavior they often justify continue to bring immeasurable suffering, destruction and death to millions of people.

To repeat, the irrational position that abortion is a sin against God because life is sacred is simply nonsense. It is a deplorable answer to the irresponsibility of a male and a female—most often a male. There is another answer!

The Social Aspects of Christianity

In the various Christian sects conforming to the dictates of the Church is more of a social function than a demonstration of moral behavior. Today, the term "Christian" may refer to one's stated beliefs but generally not to one's behavior.

While the original aim of Christianity—whose founding is credited to the Jewish tribal leader Abraham—was to assert and maintain human worth and dignity it was soon

40

subverted into a tribal identity and competed with other faiths for social and political power. Thus the numerous wars waged in the name of the Christianity over the millennia and down to modern times.

Still today most Christian sects, especially Catholicism, are basically tribal religions that serve the interests of their male founders and administrators at the expense of females and competing religions.

There is no more stark evidence of the inhumanity of a god-based religion as the invasion and conquering of the New World in the 1500s by Spanish conquistadors who believed that their Catholic religious beliefs took precedence over the cultures and lives of the millions of people who lived on the Caribbean Islands and the North and South American continents—a phenomenon that was later repeated by English and other European immigrants who began their campaigns to conquer and control—or eradicate—the Native American population in the 1600s.

In America's Civil War [1861-1865] in which hundreds of thousands of young men were killed and hundreds of thousands of others were horribly mutilated both the North and South sides publicly and loudly proclaimed that God was on their side and that they were doing God's work. Southerners justified their keeping of black human beings as slaves as in keeping with the will of God. Northerners justified their going to war as a fight against evil and sang about "God's terrible swift sword" helping them vanquish the Southern armies.

The military campaigns by the United States government against Native Americans, whom it regarded as savage pagans with few if any rights, did not end until the 1880s. It was not until 1924 that all Native Americans were "granted" citizenship by the government that had conspired in killing most of them and depriving the survivors of their homelands.

What a travesty, and what an indictment against the religious beliefs and practices of early European-Americans.

Religions Live on Ignorance

From their inceptions all of the branches of Judaism, Christianity and Islam have been based on ignorance—on the simple fact that people knew virtually nothing about the cosmos, the solar system, the Earth, the existence of thousands of other societies on other continents, and so on. And it was this prevailing ignorance over the centuries that made it possible for these religions to survive and thrive.

Not surprisingly, much of this ignorance in all of these religious sects still prevails today despite the fact that mankind has walked on the moon, astronomers study the billions of galaxies and more billions of stars in the cosmos, and scientists can literally create life.

What is equally sad is that long before the appearance of Christianity and Islam ancient Sumerian and Greek scholars and scientists had actually deduced that the Earth is a globe that is in orbit around the sun; had identified all of the inner planets out to Saturn; and had deduced that human beings evolved from lower life forms going all the way back to fish!—all knowledge lost or ignored by the time these religions were created.

A 2010 poll by the prestigious *Pew Forum on Religion & Public Life* revealed that still today American Roman Catholics and Protestants actually know very little about the history and basic tenets of their own faith. The survey revealed that atheists, agnostics, Jews and Mormons knew more about religious dogma than Catholics and Protestants.

While the United States is commonly referred to as one of the most religious nations in the world, the facts are that most Americans are ignorant not only about their own particular brand of faith they know even less about other faiths. And also not surprisingly, the lower the level of education of the individual the less he or she knew about religion. And here is a good kicker: atheists and agnostics scored the highest on the survey questions. Catholics scored the lowest.

In addition to their ignorance about things in general most so-called Christians also know almost nothing about the foundation or tenets of Islam. For an extraordinary look at the life and thought of Muhammad, the founder of Islam, see *MUHAMMAD: A Story of the Last Prophet* [HarperOne] by Dr. Deepak Chopra, his third book in a trilogy following *Buddha* and *Jesus*, all of which became bestsellers in several languages.

Quoted earlier on the difference between religions and spirituality, Dr. Chopra is the author of more than 50 best-selling books. He was born and raised in India [the scion of an elite family of doctors and military men], educated in the United States, and became a naturalized American citizen.

After getting his medical degree and practicing for several years Dr. Chopra taught at Tufts University and Boston University Schools of Medicine and served as Chief of Staff at the New England Memorial Hospital in Massachusetts and at Boston Regional Medical Center before establishing a private practice specializing in alternative medicine.

The Rebellion of Catholic Women

The sex-and-gender obsessed Catholic Church has been losing American members and priests since the political emancipation of women began in the 20th century, but it was not until female members of the cult began a concerted rebellion against its sexist practices near the end of the century that dissension within the ranks became big time.

The really Big Bang occurred in 2010 as a result of the Vatican's reaction when a number of new female priests were ordained in the U.S. and in Europe. The Vatican declared that in the eyes of God women were unfit to be priests and that ordaining them was a grave sin on the same level as the sexual abuse of young boys by priests.

In the new connected world of the Internet that absurd sexist reaction went viral within hours, resulting in the publication of data showing that most American Catholics disagree with the Vatican's anti-female views and are in favor of ordaining women.

One summary of the rebellion against the doctrines of the Church suggested that the male lords would eventually abolish the edict that male priests could not marry in an attempt to remain a relevant power in the lives of people, but the summary did not foresee the day when the Church would accept females into its male-dominated hierarchy.

That is inevitable if the Catholic Church is to survive—but in the long run it will be better for humanity if it does not survive in its present form.

A Universal Philosophy

Again, it goes without saying that god-based religions have never succeeded in performing the role they were created for: ensuring a rational and constructive standard of human behavior. Far too many of their concepts and dogmas simply did not fit the human condition even when most people had little understanding, little learning, beyond the basics of staying alive and continuing the species.

Knowledge beyond these simple basics facts of life was and is incompatible with god-based cult religions. Education will result, and should result, in the demise of all religions based on a divine Creator who supposedly watches over humanity, accepts their souls into Heaven when they die and sends them to Hell if they have broken any rules...and in the case of people don't accept Jesus

44

Christ as their Savior before dying [which, as said, is the ultimate cop-out]!*

After the death of Isa [Jesus] his followers began referring to him as Eashoa [or Yeshua] Msheekhah in Aramiac, the language of his birth. That is now translated into English as Christ the Anointed One—the word Christ coming from the Greek term khristos [chris-tos], which means "oil." But in the mindset of Christians it equates with the Son of God.

Spong's book, copiously annotated with exact quotes from the Bible, clearly reveals that the Biblical claims of the divinity of Jesus and his "miracles" are simply stories written from decades to hundreds of years later that were designed to influence ignorant people to believe that Isa did not have a biological father, despite having been born to Mary, a very human female, and was the Son of God manifested in human flesh.

Even more interesting, Spong details Biblical accounts which suggest that the reason for these stories about the birth of Isa was to cover up the fact that he was an illegitimate child. The claimed divinity of Isa did not become an article of Christian faith until long after he was executed with the willing help of his Jewish competitors who resented his popularity among the poor and oppressed. He was no doubt a great teacher who attracted followers because he taught love instead of hate; generosity instead of greed; cooperation instead of conflict—all of which were rampant in his time.

One of the great mysteries about the Biblical Jesus was where he was and what he was doing from the age of 12—when the Bible first mentions him—and the age of 34, when he showed up at the Jordan River, was baptized by John the Baptist and began a ministry that lasted for only two to three years.

There is an astounding legend in Japan—supported by documentary evidence—that Jesus and his brother Isukiri spent many these years in Japan in a village called Herai [later renamed Shingō], that he and his brother returned to Jordan when he was 34 but that it was Isukiri who was crucified by the Romans, not Jesus. The legend goes on to say that Jesus returned to Herai, married a Japanese woman, became a rice farmer, had children, and died there of old age. His tomb, and an adjoining tomb for his brother, can still be seen in Herai.

It is the position of the Jewish and Christian faiths that God and Jesus Christ are the only true sources of the wisdom that human beings must have to live decent, upright lives—a position obviously taken by the creators of these religions because up to their time people in their isolated communities had demonstrated very little enlightened intelligence.

The rules regarding charity, goodwill, honesty and other common sense things that these spiritual leaders prescribed obviously represented the ideal behavior for all human beings. They naturally appealed to most people, and attracted followers.

The trouble is fear of a vengeful God and the threat of spending eternity in Hell were not powerful enough to make everyone obey these simple dictates, resulting in Jewish and Christian leaders taking enforcement into their own hands, using a variety of cruel methods to punish both nonbelievers and turncoats.

In earlier times this historical dichotomy in Judaism, Christianity and Islam did not reduce their power over people, but with the spread of education in modern times the religions have lost much of their relevance for a large percentage of people.

There is, in fact, a deep-seated distrust and hatred for god-based religions in the conscious and sub-conscious of many people. And yet, the ideal human traits promoted by all of the religions are still very much alive and well among most people, with an astounding level of goodwill and charity among Americans and others when it comes to helping those in need.

However, it should be obvious by this time that the Biblical God of Judaism, Christianity and Islam does not watch over or take care of anyone. And it certainly doesn't do any good to credit Him for success and good luck, or to blame Him for all of the tragedies that befall mankind on a daily basis. All of these things are a result of nature doing its thing along with the good and bad freewill of individuals.

Human beings cannot become truly rational, sane and civilized until they stop depending on mythical gods and all other irrational elements of cultures, and accept full responsibility for their thoughts and actions.

Again, the answer to the question and the dilemma of human behavior is not religion. It is a universal philosophy based on a simple, rational set of rules that are culturally neutral and apply to everyone. And here the valid principles of the above religions would come into play— goodwill, no lying, no stealing, no killing, cooperation, taking care of the planet, and so on—with individuals taking personal responsibility for their behavior.

PROFIT AS THE NEW GOD

The Rise of Money Morality

The fact that Judaism, Christianity and Islam have failed in their self-declared mandates to control human behavior has allowed the rise of a new morality that is even more destructive—a new morality that was fueled by the Industrial Revolution in England in the early 1700s and was to have more far-reaching effects on human history than any other element since the development of agriculture and the creation of god-based religions.

One of the most important of these effects was that the new economy that developed over the next century was centered on profit-making as the new imperative of all businesses and government organizations, and *earning money* was the new imperative of the people who worked for them.

During the early 19th century money-and-profit-making became the economic, social and political foundations of the industrialized countries of the West. By the beginning of the 20th century all of the domestic and international affairs of the newly industrialized countries were based on the new money morality.

The perceived and real need for economic expansion, both to meet growing populations and the hunger for more economic and political power, resulted in wars becoming an even more vital aspect of public policy in a number of countries.

Among the first of these economic wars was the invasion and colonization of most of Southeast Asia and big chunks of China by European countries. In the early 1900s Japan joined the fray by invading and colonizing Korea. Then came World War I and World War II, both started by Germany to expand its economic and political clout, with Japan soon following the German example by invading China, Southeast Asia and islands in the Pacific.

At present, most of the conflicts among industrialized nations are economic rather than military. But killing and other savage actions continue on a grand scale in some countries—despite efforts by the United Nations and individual nations to stop them.

No matter how many reasons one can come up with to explain this violence the ultimate cause lies in the lack of the right kind of practical and moral education—education that programs people in the common sense attributes that

48

are the foundation of peace, goodwill, tolerance and co-operation in improving the welfare of all—all things god-based religions have failed to do.

There is virtually no area of human endeavor, including the survival and activities of religious institutions, that is not based on money.

The Excess-Consumption Time Bomb!

The profit motive has not only replaced religious-based moralities it has created an excess-consumption syndrome that is socially and spiritually insane and is like a cancer eating away at humanity and inflicting irreparable harm to the Earth.

The areas of human consumption in industrialized societies that are the most abused by the compulsion to make a profit—and are the most damaging to both humanity and the Earth—include fossil-based energy, military armaments, fashion-based wearing apparel, drugs, processed foodstuffs, alcoholic beverages, tobacco products and sugar-laden drinks.

The damage done not only to the human psyche and societies in general but also to the planet by promoting excess consumption of these and other products is incalculable in both spiritual and material terms.

This mindless drive to make a profit based on excess consumption results in most of the imagination and creative talent of mankind being used to promote the sales of products in volumes that are not related in any way to the actual needs of people.

More and more people are recognizing the stupidity and immorality of this kind of culture, but only a few have the intestinal fortitude in the first place to not fall prey to the blandishments of advertising and a social image that publicly proclaims their success in making more money than what they need to live modestly. Fewer still willingly give it up after they are caught up in the conspicuous consumption syndrome.

Americans created this lifestyle and mentality, and like a disease it has spread to other countries, particularly the newly developed and still developing countries, with China being an outstanding example.

What is incredible about the rise of China and the problems of the United States is that the Chinese approach to education, the economy and international trade as expounded by Premier Wen Jiabao in 2010 was more rational and intelligent—if self-serving—than the American approach.

In an interview with *TIME* Magazine's Fareed Zakaria Premier Wen described his political philosophy in four succinct sentences: "Let everyone lead a happy life with dignity. Let everyone feel safe and secure. Let society be one with equality and justice. Let everyone have confidence in the future."

Wen went on to say that he would strive to follow these ideals regardless of any resistance there might be from people with other political views. He added: "The wish and the will of the people is unstoppable." How's that for a definition of democracy...by a guy described as a Communist, no less!

Wen, it seems, was putting Taoism first and Communism second, i.e. Lao Tzu [604-531 B.C], the founder of Taoism, who said: "Good employers serve their workers. The best leader follows the will of the people." In reality, the leadership of China puts its own survival first and the continued growth of the Chinese economy second, despite any restraints and hardships on the population and trade conflicts with other nations.

Zakaria noted that the policies the Chinese leadership has followed since the 1980s have included building new colleges and universities, dramatically increasing the number of graduates in math and science and building an infrastructure that includes state-of-the-art airports, highways and a high-speed train network—all key parts of modernizing and internationalizing China's economy. He added that the education network the Chinese created in less than a decade is the largest in the world—an expansion Yale University President Richard Levin described as without precedent.

Zakaria went on to say that the current American attempts to get China to change the value of its currency in the expectation that it would reduce the trade imbalance is totally wrong; that in the consumption-based economy of the U.S. retail shops and chains would simply turn to the new cheap-labor countries of Asia and elsewhere to fill their shelves. The solution, he goes on, is for the United States to reform its economic infrastructure and make the necessary investments in education and training to again make the economy dynamic and its workers competitive.

Just as American business and government leaders ignored the fantastic economic progress Japan made between 1950 and 1970—during which it became the world's second largest economy—they at first ignored the fact that China began taking exactly the same steps in the early 1980s.

What an incredible example of the myopia and willful stupidity of American leaders in all fields! The once-despised Chinese Communist leaders giving Americans a lesson in capitalism! And by the end of the first decade of the 21st century China was already in the midst of its second giant leap forward: the creation of a mass market that could eventually encompasses over one billion people—a phenomenon that will have far more impact on the world than the rise of Japan.

But in creating their own economic juggernaut the Chinese leaders seem to have forgotten some of the other sage wisdom of Lao Tzu, who almost three thousand years ago wrote: "When man interferes with nature the sky

51

becomes filthy, the Earth becomes depleted, harmony with nature disappears, and creatures become extinct."

Japan was the first Asian nation in modern times to develop a mass market-based economy—between 1950 and 1965—a remarkable event chronicled in 1967 in the book, *The Japanese as Consumers—Asia's First Mass Market*, written by this author and Fred Thomas Perry.

Japan was also the first Asian nation to fall prey to the excess consumption syndrome; a cultural switch of extraordinary importance because up to 1960 the Japanese had maintained an austere but physically, emotionally and spiritually balanced life-style for over two thousand years.

This early unique Japanese lifestyle evolved from precepts contained in Shintō, their native religion, which taught respect and reverence for nature; for beauty simplified and refined down to its essence; the avoidance of conspicuous excess display, and the presence of harmony in design and style as well as in behavior.

The traditional lifestyle of the Japanese has been maintained in many areas, including shops dealing in traditional arts and crafts, restaurants featuring traditional foods, and traditional *ryokan* [rio-kahn] or inns, which still abound in the country. But for the majority of the Japanese it has been replaced by the American or Western style of living.

However, before the turn of the 21st century a growing number of Japanese began to suffer from a cultural malaise brought on by the mass consumption lifestyle, resulting in them going at least part of the way back to the simple way of living that had sustained them for millennia. For some, this included moving out of crowded urban areas into the countryside.

The whole industrialized world is challenged to follow this example to some extent—overcoming the excess-consumption syndrome and returning to a more balanced and satisfying lifestyle. This movement, although tiny, is growing in the United States, albeit slowly. Much of the future of the world depends on what China will do.

The Profit-Driven Drug Industries

The multi-billion-dollar-a-year drug industry in the U.S., both legal and illegal, has become an economic, political and social issue that is a frightening and dangerous example of the failure of basic parental responsibility, teacher responsibility, government responsibility, industry responsibility, news media responsibility, and more.

The movement toward a drug-addicted society was enhanced by the Hippie phenomenon of the 1960s—a movement that was promoted by copious news media coverage, the movie industry, and the entertainment industry.

By 2010 the market for illegal drugs in the U.S. had spawned a war in Mexico, pitting drug cartels against the government—a war that the government was incapable of winning, resulting in it beginning to consider legalizing recreational drug use—a concept highly criticized by those who pointed out that it was the market for drugs in the U.S. that fueled and financed the Mexican drug cartels.

In the United States the movement to legalize marijuana was making dramatic inroads under the guise of "medical marijuana"—a movement headed by the Medical Marijuana Project, a lobbying and information group based in Washington, D.C. that was both insidious and clever in presenting the benefits of thousands of new marijuana drugstores across the country.

Again, it was money that was driving this movement, not concern for people who had illnesses that cause permanent pain. And because dealing in drugs is extremely profitable there was no lack of money to finance the campaign.

Listening to proponents of medical marijuana—those in government as well as those on the outside—one could assume that legalizing medical pot was an opportunity to

53

create thousands of good-paying jobs and bring large amounts of tax dollars into city and state coffers.

Some Arizona politicians who were asked about the push to legalize medical marijuana suggested that it might be a good idea for the dispensaries to be run by the state. Others suggested that the dispensaries should be associated with pharmacies and other medical providers. Arizona voters approved the sale of "medical pot" in the state in 2010.

The first states to approve of medical marijuana dispensaries were California in 1996; Alaska, Oregon and Washington in 1998 and Maine in 1999. All people need to buy pot legally in states where it has been approved is a note from a doctor saying they would benefit from it. Doctors get paid for passing out these prescriptions.

Given the legal production and sale of alcohol and nicotine products it seems inevitable that marijuana will be legalized by tax-hungry states.

When the use of marijuana, heroin, meth and other drugs are added to the vast and still growing array of legal drugs sold in the United States the total is staggering. Several million people of all ages, including children, are on daily dosages of prescribed drugs…many of which have no beneficial effect whatsoever and some of which have serious side-effects.

Referring to the national epidemic of pill popping, *TIME* magazine labeled the "well-intentioned" use of drugs prescribed by regular doctors as "Addiction by Prescription."

It goes without saying that both the legal and illegal drug industries are profit-and-growth-driven…the new American morality.

There is no end to the reach and influence of the profit motive in American life. It permeates and prevails in virtually everything we do outside of pure charity work, overriding common sense and any pretense of morality.

The health insurance industry's stealth campaign to prevent health care reform, carried out by some of the country's top public relations pros on behalf of their corporate clients, was an example of the power of businesses to preserve their profit margins at the expense of the people they claim to serve.

The general public was unaware of who was behind this campaign until their identities and goals were revealed in a book entitled *Deadly Spin*, written by Wendell Potter, a former employee of insurance giant Cigna who quit his job to expose the duplicity of the campaign because his conscience got the better of him. "I had sold my soul," he told *TIME* writer Kate Pickert.

In the book Potter reveals how corporations manipulate public opinion to ensure their profits by "forming front groups, touting misleading studies and enlisting sympathetic media types to further their causes."

The reaction of the Food and Drug Administration [FDA] arm of the federal government to the appearance of e-cigarettes [electronic devices that deliver nicotine in its gaseous form] was another example of the complicity of government politicians and companies whose only aim is to make a profit without regard for the health of people.

The FDA sent a warning to five companies making the e-cigarettes that several of their health claims were not substantiated and their manufacturing processes were faulty, giving the company 15 days to report on how they would correct these failings. The FDA added that it was willing to work with the companies so that they could continue manufacturing and selling the nicotine dispensers!

Given the government's ongoing complicity with the tobacco companies to make and sell products known to kill hundreds of thousands of people a year and cost taxpayers billions of dollars, the FDA's response to the e-cigarettes was not surprising. The public rationale for such reasoning is that the Constitution prevents the government from interfering with the choices that adults make in their life-styles; in other words, if they want to endanger their lives it's up to them.

Manufacturers of both regular cigarettes and e-nicotine advertise their products to young boys and girls with insidiously clever ads that present smoking cigarettes and inhaling nicotine vapor as a smart, stylish and glamorous thing to do.

During the shocking decline of American industry in the latter half of the first decade of the 21st century the tobacco companies announced significant increases in sales and profits—much of it coming from other countries whose laws protecting their citizens are even more lax—or non-existent—than American laws.

In November 2010 I was amazed—but pleased—to see an article by syndicated columnist Richard Cohen [*Washington Post Writers Group*] entitled *Tobacco Villains Should Be Famous* in which he named the villains—the CEOs of the top tobacco companies—describing them as killers...and while he didn't do it he could have compared them to Adolph Hitler and other historic mass murderers. The headline of the article should have described these merchants of death as *infamous* not famous.

Cohen's article reminded me of another article I read in the 1960s about a Louisiana doctor who in the *1930s* announced to his interns that he wanted to show them something that was so rare they might never again see it. That something so rare was the cancerous lung of a heavy cigarette smoker.

It was also in the 1960s that a courageous lady named Betty Carnes browbeat the Arizona legislature into passing a law that prohibited hospitals from letting their patients smoke in their beds—including patients suffering from lung cancer—a first in the nation. Her husband had died of lung cancer. This prompted me to write a book about smoking and donate the first printing to a local stop-smoking program as a free giveaway.

Cohen's column did accuse the tobacco company CEOs outright of being killers who should be held accountable, and he did get it right in saying that it was the insidious amorality of the present business system that puts profit-making above the lives of people. He also labeled the board members of these huge killer combines as being equally guilty of unbelievable villainy. And then there are the stockholders who gleefully accept their cut of the profits from this deadly enterprise...and, keeping quiet behind their masks of constitutional and religious morality are the money-controlled members of Congress.

Parents and teachers should do far more to protect the young by making anti-tobacco and nicotine messages a regular part of their regular chores, as well as demanding that their political representatives on every level do everything they can to end the government-industry holocaust-like nicotine conspiracy.

A 2012 law requiring cigarette manufacturers to put graphic images of smoke-damaged lungs and other such imagery on cigarette packages was immediately attacked by powerful tobacco lobbyists and politicians from tobacco-producing states. All of the teenagers who were asked if they thought the new anti-smoking legislation would reduce the number of young people taking up the smoking habit said it would not.

There are innumerable stories relating to profit-making around the world that are also horrific, with the diamond industry centered in Africa being one incredible example. During the last years of the 20th century over four million Africans were brutally murdered in civil wars in Angola, Congo, Sierra Leone, Liberia and Ivory Coast in conflicts caused by competition in the diamond mining industry—an industry based on a product that has virtually no intrinsic value of its own but has been turned into a multi-billion dollar a year enterprise because of its concocted connection with vanity, romance and marriage.

Do no Harm! / Do Good!

It is possible to make huge profits without doing harm. In 1998 two young science grad students at Stanford University, Larry Page and Sergey Brin, talked Sun Inc. co-founder Andy Bechtolsheim into investing $100,000 in an idea they had for a new company. The company, named Google.com, was incorporated in September of that year.

Soon after Google was established the founders came up with the company slogan, "Do no Harm"—which was later adopted by a number of other companies, including some old-line firms whose motives are questionable. Within less than a decade these two young ex-science students were multi-billionaires, and represented a new breed of entrepreneurs.

Page and Brin might as well as have added "Do Good!" to their motto because the good they have done for the world is on a cosmic scale. [If you have not yet made used their free GoogleEarth service you've missed one of the technological highs of the new 21st century.]

Until most companies in the United States and elsewhere adopt a "Do no Harm! / Do Good!" corporate philosophy and live up to it the world will continue to be roiled by the profit morality and the excess consumption syndrome.

Fortunately, by the beginning of this century a growing number of people had begun talking about the need to turn away from these twin diseases, but far more people are working obsessively to get more of both.

THE BLACK HOLE
OF POLITICS

Corruption of the Political Process

The basic political system in the United States was created in a time when the overall population of the country was tiny, the number of eligible voters was smaller still, and there were far fewer power groups with their own agendas. If people really didn't like what was going on in their districts they could simply load up and move west where at first there were no political processes at all. As time passed and the populations grew money began to play an increasing role in the political system.

By the beginning of the 20th century the new money morality had infected and corrupted American culture and the political process from top to bottom. As is so glaringly obvious today people who want to participate in the governing process must buy their way into office.

Individuals running for offices who are not wealthy must raise thousands to millions of dollars to finance their campaigns. In the 2010 elections for the governorship of California candidate Meg Whitman, former CEO of eBay, spent $141 million of her own money and another $25 million in donations—apparently the record for any political candidate in the history of the country; topping 2008 presidential candidate Mitt Romney, who spent $115 million during the primary elections campaign (and lost). Whitman also lost.

That was an incredible travesty of the original political system, and a glaring example of the depths to which American culture had sunk.

By the summer of 2010 the level of political competition for power had reached new heights of immoral absurdity—a phenomenon advanced by advertising "genius" Fred N. Davis, whose forte was creating advertisements based on statements and images that were so shocking they were raw red meat for the online news media, resulting in them going viral in a matter of minutes, bringing his clients millions of dollars worth of publicity and making them virtually instant "celebrities."

Davis simply took advantage of the fact that the more outrageous an ad the more attention it will get, regardless of how inaccurate or how stupid it might be—the point being that enough of the public would end up voting for the candidates to maybe get them elected. What this had to stay about the moral character of the political figures who agreed to this approach is a good question.

The American political system is not going to reform itself. First, in most states the division of counties into political districts—which is the prerogative of state legislators—is obsolete, impractical, inefficient, unfair, undemocratic and irrational, and the system should be abolished.

As Jennifer A. Steen, a research fellow at Morrison Institute for Public Policy and an assistant professor of political science at Arizona State University said this system serves the interests of politicians instead of the people, adding: "Lines drawn by legislators reinforce the majority party's advantages or simply protects incumbents from both parties at the expense of promoting more benign goals such as partisan competition or representation for 'communities of interest' defined by shared culture, history, geography or economics."

Steen noted that in Arizona the people are empowered by the Independent Redistricting Commission [IRC] of the state to draw the district lines, and that any citizen, except politicians, can apply to become a member of the IRC. She describes the prevailing legislator controlled redistricting system as cynical and self-serving.

Residents in other states should demand that "their" legislators now in office vote for the elimination of the old district-drawing system. If they refuse, voters should vote them out of office and replace them with candidates who commit to the reform.

Second, the committee system in the federal and state legislative bodies should be abolished because it is irrational, undemocratic, unfair to the voters, and based on the power and interests of a few individuals.

All proposals should be published and distributed to both the House and the Senate and to the general public, with a set study period prior to a vote in the House and Senate—a study period that should be no less than 30 days and no more than 60 days. All proposals should be put to a vote by all members of the House and the Senate.

Failure of the Committee System

The political-party system of government as practiced in the United States is virtually bankrupt. One of its worst elements is the committee system, which has a profound influence on who gets what done. In addition to different ideologies that divide committee members on both state and federal levels the party in power gets to select the chairmen in control of the committees.

This means that instead of being a good example of the democratic process, individual committee chairmen can decide on what and when to bring up issues and they and their fellow party members almost always vote as a block.

Junior congressmen and senators who have promised their constituents that they are going to reform Washington politics when they get there have virtually no power even when appointed to committees because they generally must do the bidding of the senior party members whether they agree with them or not.

One of the first lessons that newcomers in Congress learn is that they must spend the bulk of their time raising funds for the next election.

The committee system virtually guarantees that most of the legislation introduced by members—old and new, and especially new members—goes directly into a black hole and never sees the light of day. Actually, that is not all bad!*

***

"Under democracy one party always devotes its chief energies to trying to prove that the other party is unfit to rule - both commonly succeed, and are right"—
L. Mencken, Baltimore Sun, 1930s.

***

The Two New Branches of Government!

The political system in the United States today has morphed into a kind of multi-headed monster that mitigates against common sense and rational, focused behavior. One of the reasons for this is the appearance of two new unofficial branches of government that are not by the people or for the people.

These are the far left and the far right elements of the news media and the lobbyists—both individual lobbyist who must register and account for the money they spend, and the far more powerful corporate entities from non-profits to unions that do not have to register as lobbyists and over which there are no restraints on how much money they can use to buy political influence.

The combination of the dark sides of these two unofficial branches of government poisons the political atmosphere and prevents the legal branches of government from doing the job they were designed to do.

In goes without saying that these unofficial branches of government are not going to change their spots or their behavior. It is also obvious that the influence of the lobby branch is so powerful that elected officials cannot legislate it out of business—although efforts have been made to rein it in.

That leaves it up to untainted public officials, journalists and the public at large to identify and expose the individuals, companies and organizations that have usurped the legitimate powers of the government to the point that they become ineffective and wither away. Good luck on *that!*

Ideological Conflicts

Eugene Robinson, a member of the *Washington Post Writers Group,* has enumerated key areas in the political arena in which Democrats, Republicans *and* voters act like "spoiled brats." He says it all boils down to the fact that American voters are so spoiled they demand instant, painless fixes by the government to problems that have been in the making for decades while at the same time shouting that Big Government is the problem and should be dramatically downsized, resulting in candidates and incumbents alike promising fixes they cannot deliver because the government does not have that kind of control over the causes of the problems.

Past attempts by the government to fix old economic problems and avoid creating new ones have resulted in an infrastructure of entitlements, rules and regulations that have created more problems than they have solved, are unsustainable, and are unfixable in the present political climate. Again referring to Lao Tzu, the ancient Chinese sage, he said that the more laws and rules created by leaders the more people will break them.

The reason the problems cannot be fixed is that the ideological fault lines between the old and new political parties are so wide and deep, and the self-interest of the committee and party leaders is so powerful, they refuse to compromise their positions, much less accept a good idea advanced by the other party. As Robinson says, the present situation makes no sense.

Not surprisingly, one of the major sources of ideological conflicts within the political parties are the divisions between those who want more religion in government and those who favor a totally secular government. What is politically correct for one side is political poison for the other side.

The founding fathers kept religion out of the government because they were wise enough to know that god-based religions are a form of spiritual, intellectual and social dictatorship in exact opposition to democracy—and it was the dictatorship of religions that drove the first European colonists to North America.

Demanding that a political candidate be a Christian and prove his or her Christian beliefs is a primitive throwback to the days of the Catholic Inquisition. It should be obvious to any rational individual that claiming to be a Christian is not the best measure of a man or woman...but that understanding is apparently beyond the ability of many people to comprehend. Or they are just hoping for the best.

The Voter Dilemma

To paraphrase some dry wit, political candidates, no matter how unsavory or incompetent they may be, can get elected to a public office if they can find enough fools to vote for them. And this pretty much sums up the electoral process in the United States today.

Generally, potential voters know very little if anything about the character, the competence or the background of most incumbent candidates, much less newcomers to politics. Instead of knowing enough to make wise choices voters more often than not go by the hype and crap spouted by the candidates and their handlers, and by their gender and their looks.

The figure and face of candidates are often the primary factors in their success or failure. Where candidates' names are on the ballot and the ethnic origin of their names influences many voters. Being able to talk endlessly and say almost nothing is another advantage.

In 2007 a high school teacher name David Colarusso came up with an idea for adding some common sense to the American political system. Colarusso had already created an interactive online platform called *Community-Counts* and a website called *10Questions.com* as a demonstration project.

Inspired by a group of online activists from the YouTube community, Colarusso joined forces with the YouTube group to establish the Personal Democracy Forum and complete the concept of *10Questions.com* as a cross-partisan interactive platform for voter-candidate engagement.

Together the group brought in a cross-partisan array of media partners, and officially launched *10Questions.com*, asking the public to post questions to the presidential candidates. They then invited all the candidates to post their answers, giving them all the time they needed to prepare serious answers. And then, to create a real feed-back loop and try to incentivize the candidates to avoid dodging the questions, the group invited the public to vote on whether they thought each candidate had actually answered each question.

The rationale of the creators of the site was perfectly simple and sane: instead of giving candidates 60 seconds to recite a canned answer, offer them unlimited time to prepare a serious response online. Instead of letting candidates dodge questions during live debates, create a real feedback loop and let the public vote on whether they were satisfied with candidates' answers. Instead of debates tailored for (and constrained by) the demands of broadcast television, use the interactive nature of the internet to make debates far more participatory, content-rich, and accountable.

In 2007, about 125,000 votes were cast on more than 300 questions submitted. The top 10 included questions on net neutrality, atheism, medical marijuana, warrantless wire-tapping, corporate personhood, government spending, etc.

Later, presidential candidates Edwards, Gravel, Huckabee, Kucinich, and Obama each answered at least one of the top 10 questions. Another 27,000 votes were cast judging their responses. By all accounts, *10Questions* was successful in demonstrating that an open and interactive platform for voter-to-candidate-to-voter engagement could work.

With these results the group got financial support from the John S. and James L. Knight Foundation, and retooled *10-Questions.com* to allow anyone to ask questions directly of many of the candidates seeking to represent them in the U.S. Congress, U.S. Senate, or as their state's governor.

To post and/or vote on a question, you need a Google account, as the site is powered by a souped up version of the Google Moderator question platform. No personal user information is retained, although the site allows anyone to view where questions and votes are coming from geographically, and to track the daily up-down voting on any question.

By mid-2010 *10Questions.com* covered 43 elections in 11 states, and was continuing to spread across the country, a remarkable and much needed improvement in the screwed up democratic process that came from the mind of a concerned high school teacher…not a political aspirant or a political leader.

To check what is going on in your state and the elections covered go to *10Questions.com.*

Project Vote Smart [The Voter's Self-Defense System], at www.votesmart.org, is yet another attempt to reveal the positions of candidates on issues and put them on public record so voters have some sense of where they stand. It is an organization dedicated to strengthening the most essential component of democracy—access to information—even as it suffers grave attacks from candidates and political parties, many of whom are willing to manipulate information and deceive voters.

The goal of *Project Vote Smart* interns and volunteers is to ensure that tolerance will no longer be the only option available to the millions of Americans who are tormented by the issueless rhetoric and often misleading attacks that define contemporary American politics.

The weaknesses of the America political system go well beyond what these concerned citizens and others have been voicing—and the reason they exist and have existed for so long is because the public is not educated well enough, or responsible enough, to hold politicians accountable.

Eliminating Money Politics

The only way to really reform the political system in the United States is to start by eliminating the money equation. Eliminating the hold that money politics now has on the country will require some drastic steps that only the public at large can initiate. Citizens must force their elected officials on every level of government to take the following simple steps:

1] Mandate by law that candidates cannot use paid advertisements in the news media or on signs, or have anyone else or any organization place paid advertisements on their behalf in or on any media.

2] Mandate by law that all citizens running for reelection, or election for the first time, write out in precise detail their biographical information and position on all issues that could be expected to come before them, and make their manifestos available to the public 90 days before the day of the election by releasing them to the print and electronic news media, and by printing and delivering them to voters in their districts and states.

3] Mandate by law that public campaigning by all candidates be limited to precisely 30 days before election day, and that during this 30-day period they be prohibited from basing their campaigns on criticizing their opponents.

What the Public Has to Say

Among the many critiques of Congressional representatives and senators now on the Internet as pass-on messages, the following sums up the feelings of many Americans:

A. A maxim of two 6-year Senate terms.

B. A maxim of six 2-year House terms.

C. One 6-year Senate term and three 2-Year House terms.

D. Congressional members receive a salary while in office and no pension when they leave office.

E. Congressional members (past, present & future) participate in the Social Security program.

F. All funds in the Congressional retirement fund should be moved to the Social Security system immediately. All future funds should flow into the Social Security system, and Congressional members should participate with the American people.

G. Members of Congress should purchase retirement plans, just as other Americans do.

H. Congressional members should no longer have the right to vote themselves pay raises.

I. The current health care system for members of Congress should be eliminated, and they should participate in the same health care system as other Americans.

J. Members of Congress should be required to abide by the laws they impose on the American people.

K. All contracts with past and present members of Congressmen should be voided. The American people did not make these contracts with Congressional members. They made the contracts themselves.

L. Serving in Congress was not meant to be a career. The Founding Fathers envisioned citizen legislators, serving their term(s) then going home and going back to work.

A Common-Sense Manifesto

A board of totally independent ordinary citizens, businesspeople and scholars should draw up a simple common sense manifesto of specific incremental steps to take that over a period of years that are designed fix the problems now plaguing the infrastructure of the political system, the economic system, and the education system.

To implement this manifesto the American public would have to come to its senses, stop voting on party lines, and vote for independent candidates who pledge in writing to make the changes necessary, and then hold them strictly accountable if they are elected.

Politicians already in office should be required by voters to sign off on the manifesto. If they refuse to sign the manifesto they should be blacklisted in future elections— or better yet, recalled and booted out of office.

If such drastic steps are not taken there is no hope that basic improvements will be made in the governing process.

THE ENTERTAINMENT CESSPOOL

Sex, Violence & Sleaze

As much as 75 percent of the entertainment in the U.S. is based on sex, violence and sleaze.

The most conspicuous use of sex in the United States is in promoting and selling merchandise and services of all kinds, with movies and television fare in the forefront of this incredible phenomenon.

By the mid-1900s the display of female sexuality had become one of the primary foundations of business in the United States, with several European and Hispanic countries soon following suit.

By 2005 even once sex-staid China had boarded the sex-based marketing bandwagon. The fact that it is primarily the use of *female* sexuality that primes the business pump in America and other Christianized countries is yet other outcome of the Jewish and Christian religions historically keeping women in the shadows and subservient to men—denying them the right of self-expression and making the subject of their sexuality both taboo and a subject of chronic obsessive interest among males.

In some Muslim countries the Islamic clergy has been and still is even more rigid and extreme in its efforts to keep women in virtual serfdom—a primitive practice that goes all the way back to caveman days and is just now beginning to show cracks.

Another of the results of the religious-inspired laws requiring women to keep their bodies covered is that males in these countries have developed a fetish about female breasts. Surely never in the history of mankind has more been made about any part of the human body than what is now seen in the U.S., Mexico and other countries in regards to female breasts.

You might think that an American mother being arrested for breast-feeding her baby in public has to be the epitome of stupidity. But then along comes an Islamic cleric who announces in the Iranian media that women who engage in promiscuous behavior and whose dress reveals breast-cleavage and leg not only corrupts young men and leads to adultery but is also the cause of earthquakes.

This example of religious idiocy prompted Purdue University genetics and evolution student Jennifer McCreight to create a 'Boobquake" *Facebook* group as a joke…"to help fight supernatural thinking and the oppression of women just because they showed some cleavage."

In a matter of hours over 105,000 female *Facebook* users had volunteered to join the group, resulting in news media around the world picking up on the story. The site has probably become big and profitable—with many males logging on because they think it is online pornography and they are going to see a lot of bare boobs.

What a marvelous story and what an amazing example of the power of the Internet to reveal the ongoing idiocy and stupidity of primitive religious thinking and the susceptibility of the human mind to being programmed to believe anything.

In the 20th century bras especially designed to reveal a lot of tit became big sellers. [Which was not exactly something new; at one time in merry old England women wore dresses that exposed all of their breasts…and men wore "cod-pieces" on the outside of their trousers to attract attention to their crotch areas.] By the end of the 20th century plastic surgeons [mostly males] reacting to demand from hundreds of thousands of women had turned enlarging breasts into another new industry.

But given the direction and the speed with which the breast fetish is driving "fashion" it seems safe to predict that totally bare breasts will eventually once again become so common-place in public that the breast fetish will peter out—especially the part that emphasizes huge breasts... which led a few women to have their breasts enlarged to the size of volleyballs in a move to profit from the tit obsession.

[In pre-Americanized Japan, men and women bathed together in large public bathhouses as a normal, natural thing, and women's breasts were not considered erotic— the back of the neck exposed by kimono was *the* erotic zone! But since the 1960s breasts have also become a big thing in Japan, as the Japanese became more and more under the influence of sleazy American culture.]

Interestingly, promoting prurient interest in female breasts had gone so far by the turn of the century that marketers in the fashion industry had begun to zero in on female butts as the new thing. Some of the commercials focusing on the butts of shapely females are more sexually arousing than the cleavage and breast ads because female butts are far more directly associated with actual sexual intercourse than their mammary glands.

One recent TV commercial I recall seeing focused on the butt of a man wearing tight blue jeans.

The Incredible Porn Business

The obsession with sex that is characteristic of people who have been programmed by anti-sex religions has resulted in the growth of pornography from a minor business to one of the world's largest and most profitable enterprises. First fueled by the advent of sex-based movies and television in the early 1900s, pornography went viral virtually overnight when the Internet came along.

This doesn't mean there was no porn in earlier times. Drawings, paintings and sculptures have long depicted

73

men and women in the nude and in sex acts for their arousal effects.

In fact, in earlier times cultures in some countries had large industries devoted to such things in the form of carvings, drawings and sculptures. Early Japan's famous 69-position sex charts are now collector's items worth large sums of money, and its annual sex festivals continue to attract hundreds of thousands of viewers. Sex-oriented sculptures of India, Cambodia and other Southeast Asian countries also continue to attract large numbers of tourists.

Sex-oriented novels—most of them aimed at females—began to sell by the millions in the early 1900s. By the mid-1900s printed "fuck" comics and cartoons were big things in American high schools, furtively passed around by giggling girls and smirking boys in the classrooms and hallways. [Popeye was a popular star in the cartoons!]

But it was not until cultural changes in the 1950s and 1960s had influenced and liberated movie and television producers and magazine publishers that sexual titillation became one of the biggest industries in the country and one of the foundations of the whole economy.

Visual and verbal pornography are now a mainstay of the movie and television industries. Even the broadcast news media has joined the sexual titillation crowd by selecting sexy female newscasters who are groomed fit to kill, wear short skirts revealing a lot of leg, and flirt with both guests and viewers.

As of this writing films showing both partial and complete nudity are now common fare on some television channels. Sexual intercourse showing [depicting] everything except the entry of the male penis into the female vagina is common. For a small fee you can access the real hard stuff on any TV set.

In addition to the huge personal, individual market for hard-core pornographic films—delivered on television, on

DVDs and so on—many hotels around the world have been on the porn profit-wagon since the 1970s.

Their very transparent rationale is that their guests deserve to have a choice in what they watch on television when in their rooms. The bottom line is, of course, staying on a par with other hotels in order to protect their profit margins.

As incredible as it seems on the surface, the right to produce, distribute and sell pornography is protected by the "Freedom of Speech" provision in the American Bill of Rights…a right repeatedly reaffirmed by the Supreme Court of the United States and buttressed by an army of lawyers paid by pornographers.

In the 1970s *Hustler* magazine publisher Larry Flynt had an attorney on a $15,000 a month retainer to fight off lawsuits if and when they occurred. This monthly expense was probably next only to the cost of printing the magazine but it was pocket change to the publisher. Despite the unsavory media-created reputation Flynt had as a smut peddler, he had goals that were more admirable than those claimed by many religions. His aim was to force people to be honest and aboveboard about their prejudices and sex obsessions, face them, and overcome them. He knew his approach was shocking to the average person. He also knew absolutely that it would make him immensely rich, but he was honest about it.

Again, the incredible market for porn was not created by the pornographers. It was created by the religious teachings that sexual behavior outside of marriage and not for the purpose of procreation was a sin against a vengeful god and those guilty of ignoring these teachings would go to Hell.

To prevent men from being aroused and seduced by females the religions mandated that women keep their bodies covered and not engage in any kind of licentious behavior. In some societies the sanctions against these mandates included death—a sick male response still in force in some Islamic communities.

The very successful efforts of religions to deny, ignore and subvert both male and female sexuality naturally resulted in males becoming pathologically obsessive about female sexuality.

Male pornographers are not the only ones who take advantage of this cultural aberration. Since women are naturally smarter than men, some who are liberated have also taken advantage of the male obsession with female sexuality to create their own porn sites.

Porn Tycoons & Religions!

People who are profiting from pornography—some of whom have become billionaires—should bow down several times a day to the God-based religions—Judaism, Christianity and Islam—that have misunderstood and abused human sexuality since their inception, resulting in most of humanity becoming obsessed with sex, with sexual genitalia, with everything that has to do with sex.

Despite claims to the contrary, it is sex that runs the world, not love. And as long as the sexual nature of human beings is denied, ignored and suppressed, and people are punished for breaking the religious taboos designed to dramatically limit sexual expression, the obsession is not going to go away.

In other words, the profit morality will continue to prevail... at the expense of the religious elements that in fact are rational and humane but cannot compete with the power of the sexual nature of humanity.

The Traditional Sex Trade

The traditional sex trade itself is, of course, one of the world's largest and most enduring industries, even though it continuously inflicts immeasurable suffering on millions of young girls and women.

Not surprisingly, the business of sex has long been fodder for the news media, which periodically covers it like any other news category but never gets down to the nitty-gritty of why the industry continues to flourish on such a massive scale.

Selling and buying sex also periodically gets the attention of politicians and religious leaders who routinely decry its presence, but they too ignore the underlying reasons for its existence. And as is well known, many of them participate in the action themselves, although they try to keep it secret.

You might think that there is some kind of conspiracy going on—a worldwide conspiracy that both allows and protects the sex industry from serious interference by anyone or any organization. And you would be right.

The conspiracy is as ancient as the industry itself, and is an outgrowth of the natural sexual instincts of males to have sexual relations with females on a regular basis—and to have sexual access to more than one female whenever possible.

As noted earlier, this predatory sexual nature of males is a built-in characteristic that is a fundamental part of the survival instinct of all organic life forms. In human males this drive can be so powerful it prevents them from thinking and behaving rationally, and when it is denied and/or repressed bad things can happen.

In males sexual energy builds up like a battery being charged. When the energy in the "sex battery" of males is not dispelled by having intercourse (or masturbating) it begins to have a negative impact on them. Their thinking and their behavior changes, and those with more powerful sex drives often resort to some kind and degree of violence to obtain sexual release. [Masturbation only partially relieves the sex energy buildup.]

Females are also genetically imbued with a survival instinct and are driven to attract males to impregnate them, but from the first days of the human species they were under the control of males who were superior in size and strength, and they were subject to being severely punished if not killed if they did not accommodate males who approached them. Both males and religions have traditionally prevented females from understanding and acting on their own sexual needs.

As the human species advanced intellectually and began to form larger and larger groups it gradually became customary in most societies for the male rulers and their male-priest allies to establish rules that limited most men to one wife at a time, or prescribed the maximum number of wives they could have—a movement that totally ignored the sexual nature of most males and all females.

As is also well known, in many societies these limitations did not apply to the rulers and top officials, resulting in concubine and mistress-keeping become common among the ruling elite and the wealthy minority (who were invariable aligned with the political and religious leaders). The Bible notes that the famous King Solomon—the leader of a relatively small Jewish tribe—had 700 wives and 300 concubines. This sounds like a far-out exaggeration meant to burnish Solomon's manly image, but such numbers are a matter of historical record in a number of cultures.

But whatever the society and whatever social system it had, a large number of men always ended up without the opportunity for regular sexual release. And, of course, many who had wives simply gave in to the urge to have extra-marital sex. These factors, combined with the material and security needs of many females and their families, led to the early development of sex as a trade.

In some societies religious leaders recognized and accepted the true nature of men, and created a system in which men—married or single—could have sex with female priests and acolytes. [Interestingly, Hawaiians had

78

separate "sex houses" for royalty and for commoners that featured a variety of sex games. One game for commoners consisted of bowling for sex—rolling a wobbly coconut across a floor toward a lineup of females to select a partner for the night...surely hoping it would go to one that was attractive.*

---

*This custom was banned by American missionaries when they arrived in Hawaii only a few years after the islands were discovered by English seafaring explorer James Cook in 1778. If Hawaii ever runs short of tourists all it would have to do is restart the bowling-for-sex game.

Obviously, political, social and religious leaders have never resolved the sexual nature of males or females, which explains why the sex trade has survived into modern times. In short, it serves the purpose and needs of many men, and, in a perverse way, some women.

As is well known, law enforcement agencies in the U.S. periodically attempt to keep the sex trade behind closed doors, typically targeting females instead of males, even though the trade caters almost exclusively to males.

As the cultural restraints against extra-marital sex and consensual sex among singles weaken, the need for commercial sex may diminish, but it will not go away in the foreseeable future; not as long as so many men need—or think they need—the services the trade provides.

The only way that the sex trade could be dramatically and quickly reduced in size would be the mandatory state-enforced use of chemicals to block the natural sex drive of men. This will not happen as long as males are in control.

The "natural solution" that seems to be developing is a simple sexual free-for-all situation that is culturally approved as long as it is consensual.

This is an area of human behavior that the education system must eventually address in a rational, honest and humane way, beginning with middle school students, because parents cannot or will not do it.

The Violence Syndrome

The incidence of violence in the United States and other countries today might seem to be a new low in the history of humanity but that is not the case. The variety and volume of violence has increased exponentially with population growth and new ways to harm and kill but violence is built into the genetic makeup of human males.

Extreme violence has played a major role in the story of mankind, becoming institutionalized with the appearance of states and religions, both of which have traditionally depended upon violence to survive and thrive.

The dehumanization, brutalization and slaughter of some eight million Jews by the Nazis during World War II had too many precedents in history to count. It was just the volume and the filmed evidence of the holocaust that made it so shocking.

Incredibly, in the 1960s the American movie industry began to use brutality and extreme depictions of violence to increase the popularity and profitability of its films. In no time, the surefire fix for a successful movie was violence and sex, and that combination transitioned into video games for children.

From the 1980s on all Americans who viewed and/or listened to public entertainment were fed a diet of violence.

The third factor in the growth of the entertainment industries from the 1960s on was the introduction of verbal sleaze—of language that was designed to shock. By the first decade of the 21st century, "fuck you," "fucking this" and "fucking that" had become a conspicuous part of the dialogue of both male and female entertainers…with some newscasters beginning to use such terms as "the F word," in a move in the same direction.

Not surprisingly, the news media were major partners in the spread of entertainment based on violence, sex and sleaze.

Entertainers & Drugs

The use of so-called recreational and medicinal drugs in the United States is a threat to the nation. The fact that it has been allowed to develop to this point is a national disgrace and should get money-oriented businesses, parents, teachers, educators and elected officials who are responsible for letting it happen indicted as accessories to a crime.

The rampant use of recreational drugs in the United States took off in the late 1950s and early 1960s, first promoted by so-called Hippies, "rock" musicians and counter-culture news media. It quickly spread to other entertainers, particularly to young people in the movie and television industries, and finally to students all the way down to the 7th and 8th grade levels of elementary schools.

Well before the end of the 20th century recreational drug use in the United States had become a multi-billion dollar a year industry, involved hundreds of thousands of people, and was a national tragedy that business and political communities could not resolve. The problem has continued to grow simply because of the money-morality and corruption that now pervades American culture.

Not surprisingly, substance abuse has generally been highest among young males in the lowest income and educational brackets—Blacks and Hispanics—but millions of Whites from middle and upper class families have also given in to the seductive power of getting high on drugs, primarily because of the influence of the entertainment industries.

The New Drug Lords

Major pharmaceutical companies are also big players in this American tragedy, spending billions of dollars a year on television, in print media and on the Internet hyping drugs they claim will cure all of the ailments, complaints and problems that people have—from bad complexions, hair loss, obesity and sexual dysfunctions to getting old—creating an environment in which taking drugs is a natural and necessary part of life.

The world's largest and most dangerous drug lords are not Mexican or Columbian. They are American; they are the heads of the huge drug companies and their doctor distributors who are all licensed to engage in the drug trade. George Orwell's frightening novel *1984*, in which the government conspired to get the whole country addicted to drugs, got it right.

Given the history of the United States it now seems inevitable that the only action the government can and eventually will take is to make the use of marijuana—the most commonly used illegal drug—legal and tax it, the way it did to alcohol and tobacco when it lost the ability to control these substances—both of which are more harmful and more destructive than pot.

Blame for this incredible situation also falls on parents, educators and politicians—some of whom were part of the problem because they were among the pot-smoking generations. Far too many of them still today stand by and watch silently as the entertainment media aimed at the young hype the use of drugs among handsome, well-to-do and successful people in attractive sensually oriented settings.

When in 2010 the Mexican government began giving serious consideration to legalizing pot as its only way of getting the drug-related murders, bribery of government officials and law enforcement members under control, the president of Mexico made the obvious point that unless the

United States—the largest market for the drug—also made pot legal, making it legal in Mexico would not work.

The Marijuana High

By 2010 the movement to make marijuana available to virtually anyone who wants to indulge was fast becoming a reality, resulting in a marijuana rush that spread around the world, making it inevitable that marijuana growers and sellers would proliferate at lightning speed. Marijuana cultivation was already the largest cash crop in the state of California.

TIME magazine made the main-streaming of marijuana its cover story in the 22 November 2010 issue, running an article by Andrew Ferguson of the *Colorado Times* which detailed the well-financed Colorado-based campaign to give marijuana a new feel-good image that conjured up such things as apple pie and ice-cream.

This clever campaign used a variety of euphemisms for pot that make it sound like a medicine, and described how one really savvy seller had created a number of "infused products," including 100% organic lemon bars that are soaked in marijuana concentrate.

Given the fact that most people can be programmed easily and quickly to believe almost anything, the success of the campaign was virtually inevitable.

THE ADVERTISING CONSPIRACY

Serving the Profit God

Product, service and entertainment advertising has become a cancer eating away at the physical, mental and spiritual health of mankind—all in the name of profit.

The American advertising industry has long been looked upon as one of the bulwarks of both the democratic and the capitalistic systems that have defined the United States since the early 1800s. It goes without saying that both of these systems have made extraordinary contributions to the wealth and welfare of Americans, but there have always been elements in these systems that were destructive and harmful, and these insidious elements have grown with time.

In earlier times advertising was important in bringing the existence and benefits of products and services to the attention of as many people as possible so they would know where to buy them if they needed them. From around the 1950s and 60s the manufacturing and service industries became so competitive that the role of advertising gradually switched to beating out the competition, to inducing people to buy more than what they needed, and to buying things they didn't need...in other words attempting to ensure that the companies not only survived but made a profit above and beyond what the market would normally provide them.

One of the most negative aspects of advertising today is that a great deal of it is aimed at children and teenagers, and is fiendishly clever, subversive and harmful.

The advertising industry's insidiously sophisticated selling of sugar-laden cereals and other foods to children sets them up for obesity. Glamorizing alcoholic drinks to teens and adults and getting millions of people habituated to drugs they don't need...some of which have serious side effects...costs Americans billions of dollars annually.

One of the examples of the power of the news media and advertising to glamorize and popularize a new product was the appearance of new drink called *Adult Chocolate Milk,* which is chocolate milk laced with vodka. The new 40-proof vodka drink was created by a 38-year old California mom in 2009 after she gave her kids regular chocolate milk before putting them to bed. She then added vodka to her own chocolate milk drink, and announced on her *Facebook* site that she was enjoying "some adult chocolate milk." The online response was extraordinary, and led to a new enterprise that soon added Adult Orange Cream, Adult Fruit Punch and Adult Limeade to its product line.

Clever advertising and a sensual bottle-design contributed to the news media picking up on the story and making the new drink sound like an antidote for all of the economic concerns and problems associated with being an adult by returning people to their carefree childhood days.

Another serious side effect of advertising is its contribution to women who become pregnant overeating and gaining from 20 to 50 or more pounds than they should, affecting their un-born fetuses and setting them up for a lifetime of being over-weight if not obese. [Most Chinese, Filipino, Malaysian and other Asian women who have had as many as nine children remain as slender as teenagers.]

Advertising aimed at children and teens ignores common sense and undercuts the little parental control remaining to induce the young to eat and drink things that are bad for their health and will adversely affect the rest of their lives. It encourages other behavior that ranges from mental and physical harm to the individual to further degrading cultures that are already in the gutter.

While the causes of this phenomenon are well known they are so deeply entrenched in the profit-oriented culture that they cannot be easily or quickly eradicated.

But if an effort to eliminate this disease is not made—by parents and teachers—the negative impact on the health and functioning of the young will continue to grow, further degrading the culture. There are even more areas of advertising aimed at adults that are contributing to the degeneration of the culture in general—from the education problem to the degradation of the Earth's environment.

The Excess-Consumption Disease

By the end of the 20th century aggressive profit-driven advertising had created an excess-consumption syndrome that prevailed throughout the American economy and had begun spreading throughout the economies of other industrialized nations. It has now reached the point that it has destroyed much of the rational thought process, and controls much of the mindset and behavior of a growing percentage of the Earth's population.

There would appear to be no remedy for this insidious virus other than for parents, teachers and administrators who perceive of the dangers inherent in this situation to slowly but steadily introduce into the basic education of children the insidious nature of the system and a new value system based on real, actual, rational needs that would eventually result in the excess-consumption syndrome disappearing in conjunction with a balanced economic system.

It is not going to disappear any time soon but by 2010 there was a glimmer of hope. The news media began reporting on the appearance of a small movement among the economically depressed population to downgrade their consumption habits and expectations—not as a deliberate choice, however, but because of the economic situation. Some of these people were reported as saying that having and consuming less freed them and made them happier than they were before—both common sense and very old wisdom.

The Incredible Obesity Epidemic

Another cultural failure resulting from a combination of the power of food manufacturers, their advertising agencies, and the willful stupidity of parents in particular and adults in general, is the epidemic of obesity in the United States. The sight of huge numbers of men and women who weigh from 300 to 500 pounds or more waddling around like giant over-inflated character balloons is grotesque to say the least.

The number of children and adults who are obese is a national disgrace and should be a national scandal. But there has been a conspiracy among food producers, food outlets, their advertizing agencies, and the medical fraternity to both justify this incredible situation and to blame the individuals for overeating. Some medical experts are on record as saying that obesity is not the fault of every obese person, claiming that it is genetic, which actually appears to be partly true, since fat mothers give birth to unusually large babies who appear to inherit a propensity to become obese.

This incredible malady has resulted from both the willful stupidity of parents and people in general and the business obsession with making profits no matter what the cost to the public. The only permanent cure is education over a period of a generation.

And that means a lot of people—parents, teachers, administrators and politicians—have to join forces to make anti-obese programming a standard part of education. Is that ever going to happen? Don't bet on it being soon. Too many unconscionable people have too much self-interest at stake. If it has any chance of happening within a generation it will take the combined force of an army of champions who will not relent in accusing and shaming and suing leading perpetrators who are responsible for this pathological predicament. This includes many doctors.

As noted above, new research indicates that obese mothers give birth to babies that are heavier than normal, and that these babies inherit from their mothers some kind of genetic switch that predisposes them to overeat and become obese and to develop a number of ailments that are associated with being overweight—another reminder of Albert Einstein's comment that the stupidity of human beings is infinite.

In 2010 it was estimated by the National Bureau of Economic Research that the annual cost of obesity was 168 billion dollars, which amounted to about 17 percent of all medical costs.

Finally in late 2010, following a national anti-obesity campaign by First Lady Michelle Obama, President Barack Obama, signed into law a nutrition bill designed to promote healthier foods in free school lunches.

The Fashion Craze Example

While it may appear to be inconsequential, the influence of the designer fashion world, particularly in apparel for females of all ages, is another factor in the decline of common sense and the ascendancy of profit over the welfare of people and the planet. The impact of excess spending on fashions impacts on the whole culture, including education. In the U.S. billions of dollars are wasted annually by individuals and families in an effort to keep up with the year's fashions.

Despite the fact that the fashion industry provides employment for millions of people it is inherently irrational and wrong.

Not surprisingly, the fashion world is based on using sex to market both its female and male fashions, with special emphasis on the obsessive lure of sex in its female fashions—a practice that has, of course, spread to other industrialized countries.

Fashion shows held in New York, Paris, Rome, Tokyo and other major capitals are very much like sex peep shows used to be. These highly promoted displays have a fundamental and direct impact on the attitudes and behavior of people, especially on the young, adding to the excess-consumption syndrome.

The Global Battle for Resources

The emergence of Japan, South Korea, Taiwan, Hong Kong, Singapore, China, India and Russia as consumer markets, combined with the American excess-consumption syndrome that quickly affected the middle-class and well-to-do in these nations, has dramatically increased the competition for the world's natural resources.

The battle for global resources is not a recent phenomenon. It began after the Industrial Revolution in the 1700s, when the Spanish, Portuguese English, French and other Europeans began scouring the world for resources to feed their industries and their new appetites, beginning a colonization era that was to lead to a long list of invasions and occupations that was to remake the world.

By the late 1990s there was a new kid on the block: China, which was well on its way to becoming the world's largest importer of natural resources. Beginning in the early 1970s Chinese leaders began mapping out programs designed to not only allow China to compete with other industrialized countries economically and politically but to surpass them—an unstated move to return China to its glory days when it was the Central Kingdom and all other nations within its vicinity were tributaries.

The expansion programs initiated by China went further than just education. In conjunction with allowing the first foreign companies to start doing business in China the government made it a policy to require American, Japanese and other foreign companies wanting to get into the Chinese market to make some or all of their technology available to the government and/or their Chinese partners.

In addition to this policy, which saw the transfer of billions of dollars worth of technology to China, the Chinese government also initiated a major spy program designed to ferret out American technology. High tech piracy continues to be rampant in China, and by 2010 there were fields in which Chinese technology was superior to American technology.

You could say that China's leaders saw it as the new Rome, which in its heyday ruled most of Europe and huge areas of the Near East. This Chinese drive was not aimed at turning the rest of the world into colonies in the traditional sense. It was aimed at assuming political leadership in the areas that count and in gaining and keeping control of the raw materials it needs to feed its growing industries.

By 2010 the inroad China had made into several African nations in tying up natural resources was remarkable. State-owned enterprises combined business deals with financing, engineering and building highways, railways, and other infrastructure that these nations sorely needed... and were not forthcoming from American and other Western companies.

And these advances were not only in African nations that were friendly to the U.S. and the West. They included nations that the United States and some of its Allies did not do business with for political reasons, from Myanmar and North Korea to Sudan.

According to 2010 forecasts, China will be the primary trading partner of over 100 countries by 2040. Several countries were already totally reliant on China for their economic stability.

And just as Japan did in the early 20th century and South Korea did from the 1960s on China's state-owned companies and private companies have a major campaign of sending staff overseas to learn the languages and cultures of the countries they do business with and want to do business with. In many cases, the individuals sent abroad have no work duties at all; their only responsibility being to learn the languages and the cultures—a system the Japanese originated in the 1870s and repeated in the early and mid-1900s, and American companies still do not do.

Another incredible element in the present industrial system is the fact that competing industrial nations spend billions of dollars buying raw materials from undeveloped countries, such as Congo in Africa, where a the time of this writing the bulk of the money goes to warlords who use it to maintain armies and buy arms to keep themselves in power and oppress the people.

In Congo alone United Nations statistics show that over five million Congo tribe members—men, women and children—have been murdered, and hundreds of thousands of girls and women have been raped by soldiers. UN surveys in South Africa report that 37 percent of the adult males admit to having committed rape.

What a terrible indictment of the human race—not to mention the self-appointed keepers of human morality and their failure to prevent such things! And the root of this as well as other human problems is the failure of male-made cultures to cope with real human needs.

A New Universal Strategy

Of course, it goes without saying that a universal strategic plan is needed to address all of the economic needs of all countries on an equitable basis. However, this is a concept that brings into play all of the ancient and primitive characteristics of human beings—tribalism, territorialism, religious differences, races and colors, along with past history, present situation, territorial size, population, location, and so on.

This means it will not be resolved in the foreseeable future by plan and by action because some or all of the larger more powerful nations will put their priorities high on the list if not first. This means the evolution from competition to cooperation with have to come about in slow incremental steps.

It might not come about at all if there is not a concerted effort among the large and powerful nations to incorporate the concept of a shared world into their education systems, to wean their populations off of the ancient prejudices, the old animosities and the selfish instincts.

THE NEWS MEDIA VIRUS

Adapting to the New Profit Morality

Like all other areas of the American economy the mantra and the imperative of the news media has always been to make a profit. But with the advent of the Internet making it possible for virtually anyone to become a news source the collapse of news media standards in the pursuit of profit was inevitable.

The negative influence of today's news media is incredible. It is blatantly obvious and getting worse by the day. It adversely affects virtually every area of life—socially, economically, politically and spiritually—and despite all of the hemming and hawing by people who recognize its destructive influence, it continues to make a mockery of common sense, rationality and any pretense of positive morality.

And this whole morass derives from the misuse of the Constitutional provision regarding freedom of speech to advance the fortunes of individuals; to make money in total disregard for the damage it causes—not to mention the obvious idiocy that is often involved—one example being a craze among young women for tattoos.

During the heyday of the so-called Hippie Movement in the 1960s it became vogue among both young men and women to get tattoos to demonstrate their rebellion against Establishment values and customs. This rebellion was primarily voiced and advanced by songs and music that broke all of the old taboos against vulgar behavior and dress—something that appealed directly to the very young on a subconscious level.

Profit-oriented movie and television producers joined this rebellion and began to promote the same ideas and behavior that had grown out of the Hippie Movement—outlandish fashions, female nudity, unrestricted sexual activity, tattooed anti-heroes and gratuitous violence...all of which are now as American as apple pie.

Just one small part of this rebellion was the growing incidence of tattoos among young girls after the Hippie Movement had faded into the background—something that just a generation earlier would have been unthinkable. By the first decade of the 21st century the news media had begun to cooperate with entrepreneurial tattoo artists to promote tattoos as an "in" thing to do, with national tattoo organizations and annual "tattoo festivals."

This tattoo phenomenon can be blamed on the failure of parents and educators to instill sensible values and common sense into the mindset of the young—not to mention that copious body decorations have historically been associated with small tribes of people still on the savage level who used it as a tribal marker, and in more modern times with biker gangs, low ranking sailors, marines and soldiers.

The Black Hole of Competition

A huge portion of the daily, weekly and monthly print news media in the United States abrogated any pretense of standing for and upholding a rational level of moral behavior when their existence was threatened by competition from broadcast and online news media as well as other print media. They lowered their standards or they died.

This corruption is especially glaring and conspicuous in the manner in which these publications report on and hype the entertainment industries that specialize in content based on soft and hard pornography, violence and sleazy behavior in general—much of which is aimed at young people, including children.

Very good writers in publications that once stood for honesty and integrity now utilize their skills to cleverly hawk the movies, television shows, video games and books that in another time and another place would be banned.

Public relations professionals hired by companies and individuals, along with gossip columnists published by newspapers and magazines, are also guilty of using their well-honed talents to promote ill-advised products and agendas by encasing them in an aura of integrity, value and glamour.

Comic strips in newspapers and comedians on television have become social commentators with agendas of their own, subtly making anti-social and anti-human behavior sound like okay fun. Film makers inject political agendas into movies promoted as entertainment.

There are still honest and forthright journalists and publications in the news media field, but their numbers are dwindling and the cacophony erupting from their anything-that-will-sell competitors mostly drowns them out.

The primary force in the motivation and goals of most of America's professional news media today is simply to get as much of the spoils of war as they can. Some publications have simply eliminated any restraints or standards on what they publish.

The Insidious Enemy Within

The widespread disappearance of integrity among members of the news media of America has resulted in many of these journalists, commentators and columnists becoming the equivalent of a war-time 5th column—spies and saboteurs—whose misinformation and slanted "news" has negative and destructive effects on the country at large.

Unlike spies and saboteurs, however, most of these individuals and enterprises do not work under cover. They are out in public with as big a bang as possible, and the more notice they get and the more they are criticized, the more they like it because that attracts larger audiences and they get paid more by the advertisers that sponsor them.

The insidious power of these elements in the press is virtually unbounded. They can and do control the attitudes and behavior of millions of people.

One telling example of this insidious element in American culture is the review of books, films and video games by magazines, newspapers and the broadcast media. Because the media gets, or wants to get, advertising from the creators of these products they cater to them by hyping their books, films and games no matter how damaging the influence of the content may be to children and adults alike. At a rough estimate, some 70 to 80 percent of these products add to the sleaze that now characterizes American culture.

Most of these reviewers, being professional writers who still have a smidgeon of conscious, make an effort to disguise the more salacious and gutter-level content of the products they cover with clever writing that acknowledges its presence and serves to promote their sale. Examples of this are rampant in every issue of many newspapers and magazines.

A typical example of the power of the press to affect the lives of people and the security of nations on a national and international level occurred during this writing.

An anti-Islam pastor of a tiny [about 50 members] "World Peace Outreach Center" in Florida announced on *Facebook* that he was going to stage an "International Burn-a-Quran Day" [the Quran being the Islamic holy book and itself considered divine and sacred by Muslims].

The American press picked up on the story and spread it around the world, causing a flap that reached to the highest levels of the American military, the White House and, of course, Muslim nations around the world.

As typical, hundreds of print and broadcast journalists spent hours and days feasting on this burning threat, turning it into one of the biggest stories in the world, resulting in demonstrations and riots in some Muslim countries and a number of deaths.

The news media perpetrators of this phenomenon distanced themselves from putting the lives of people in danger by claiming that the democratic principle of the "right to know" takes precedence over ignoring a story—and that was all they needed.

Several days after the news feast began syndicated columnist Michael Gerson [*Washington Post Writers Group*] did a clear-eyed piece that put the whole scam into its proper perspective. He began his column with:

"It is a horrifying wonder of the Internet Age that a failed, half-crazed Florida pastor with a *Facebook* account can cause checkpoints to be thrown up on major roads in New Delhi, India, provoke violent demonstrations in Logar province south of Kabul, Afghanistan, and be rewarded with the attention of America's four-star commander in Afghanistan and the president of the United states."

Gerson then added that the event was part of the globalization of insanity, and the culmination of the revolutionary logic of radicals that the "propaganda of the deed"—usually violent acts—can be powerful enough to inspire the masses to topple nations.

In the end, the Anti-American demonstrations abroad, the intervention of the president of the United States and other top leaders resulted in the cult leader cancelling the Quran burning, but the clever pastor got what he wanted from the news media.

There should be some kind of constraints to prevent the press from turning undeserving people, some with dangerous ideas, into celebrities—something that has become a regular feature in American culture.

But that, according to Gerson, is not likely to happen because the Internet has not only made attention for stupidity a democratic right it has made it possible for the most outrageous lunatics to have their voices heard around the world in a matter of seconds—both a first in the history of the world.

The Unfixable!

In the present contexts of American culture any hope of returning integrity and responsibility to the news media is not possible. It will continue as it is as long as it is both supported and driven by the overall culture of the country. Like education, it is not an isolated problem. It is a symptom of the obsession to make money.

CULTURAL SABOTAGE

The Insidious Newspeak

Revolutionaries, religious leaders and political ideologues have always used culturally pregnant terminology to advance their causes—new words that they created or old words that they gave new meaning to—some of them so effectively that over a period of time they changed the course of world history.

Beginning in the early 1900s new communications technologies—starting with the radio—gave people in the above categories the ability to repeat their messages over and over and influence large numbers of people virtually instantly.

The advent of the Internet gave these users the ability to reach as many as a billion people with the push of a few buttons. By the end of the 20th century large numbers of popular radio and television commentators and others were filling the air with messages designed to change the meanings of words to advance their goals.

This movement was based on using the technique of newspeak—applying new meanings to old words—that was one of the foundations of the frightening novel *1984* by George Orwell, in which the government took control of the minds and behavior of the people by manipulating words and their meanings, and keeping them quiet by getting them hooked on drugs.

Redefining what is Right & Wrong

Among the examples of present-day newspeak: such terms as "undocumented immigrants" in reference to illegal aliens, and "Islamic fundamentalists" instead of Islamic terrorists. Both of these newspeak terms are designed to change the way people think about and react to illegal immigrants and terrorists.

Another very conspicuous and powerful example of newspeak relates to marijuana. In the first decade of the 20th century very clever advocates of making marijuana available to anyone who has or claims to have some kind of body pain stopped using "smoking pot" and began using such terms as medicine, medicate, caregivers and patients in reference to smoking marijuana instead of the pejorative pot and potheads.

The purveyors of such newspeak are aided and abetted, both knowingly and unwittingly, by the news media, which thrives on the frightening, the lurid, the sensational, and the shocking.

The mindset and behavior of all people are controlled by key words in their native language, and spin masters who control the meaning and use of key words control the people. Religious leaders were among the world's first word spin masters.

Today's main spin masters—academics, radio and television commentators, politicians and others who have political and economic agendas—run their campaigns under the guise of political correctness, and castigate those who disagree with them as being un-American if not traitors.

Entertainers, including video game producers and hip-hop singers, are masters at reprogramming the mindset of preteens and teenagers, overriding whatever lessons and values they may have learned or should have learned from their parents and teachers.

Subverting Cultural Traditions

The influence of the word spin masters reaches into all areas of American life, from basic ethics to political beliefs and the education process. Like religious leaders, they know that the constant repetition of beliefs and concepts combined with ritualistic behavior works like magic in programming the minds of people who have not been taught or developed critical thinking—a circumstance that especially applies to children, young people and the uneducated, and therefore applies to the majority of the population.

The reason for this cultural weakness is, of course, the historical failure of both religious and secular education to teach logical reasoning and common sense.

Lack of a Philosophical Foundation

One of the reasons why Americans are so easily seduced into extreme left and right political and religious positions is that we do not have a solid philosophical base for our education systems, our economy or our politics—a lack that has profound implications for the future.

Political philosopher and Harvard University Professor Michael Sandel has been teaching and writing about the vital importance of all areas of human life having a philosophical foundation since the 1990s.

Prof. Sandel posits his theme in terms of justice and moral behavior without emphasizing the word philosophy—perhaps because people understand these terms better and often think of philosophy as not being relevant to everyday life. He also directly relates the role of philosophy/justice in sustaining democratic principles, and in judging the market system and the financial markets—voicing serious concern about market-oriented societies and governments.

A glaring failure of the market system emphasized by Prof. Sandel is the growing gap between the rich and the poor. He says this inequality raises questions about justice and the meaning of a just society, and he faults the country's education systems for not emphasizing civic studies that would make students better citizens able to engage in the serious public debate necessary to reform the political system. He adds that the news media should be equally responsible for providing forums in which this debate can take place. He sums up by saying that citizens have to demand better politics before politicians will give it to them.

PARENTAL FAILURES & FIXES

The Education of Parents!

Improving the American education system is not that simple because in many cases the parents themselves are the basic problem. An extensive survey of parents and children in 2010 reconfirmed what was already obvious. Many parents take very little interest and spend very little time providing their children with the basic education they should have before they start to school. In many cases these parents don't have the time to teach their children because they work long hours. In other cases they themselves lack the necessary education. Some simply opt out of the responsibility for selfish reasons, leaving it up to schools.

Another cultural failure that impacts directly on the education of huge numbers of American children is the fact that their mothers are single, became pregnant when in their mid-to-late teens and know little or nothing about how to properly parent a child. This is a cultural failure of the parent or parents of these single teenage mothers...and the blame goes back at least another generation.

Families in which the male member is a step-father or live-in boyfriend often have even more serious problems, with physical abuse of the children being common, including cases of serious injury and death. In some such families the adults wage war against each other, using the children as pawns.

Since many parents lack either the will or the ability to teach and mentor their children for today's world a step in the right direction would be to require first-time parents to attend indoctrination sessions on how to prepare their children for school before a school will allow them to enroll their kids.

All parents should be required to present schools with an honest, detailed report of any educational process their children have undergone before their first school year, and with an even more honest report on their character and personality—from the games they like to play to what upsets them. Only parents can truly and quickly evaluate the weak and strong points of their children, and if they don't inform their teachers both the teachers and children are disadvantaged.

I'm Angry! Aren't You?

To say that parents in general are fed up with the weaknesses and failings of the education system is putting it mildly. Here is what parent Carolyn Spencer (who adds that she remains "hopeful") had to say:

> "I am a pushing-60 baby boomer and a 'delayed' parent, so my daughter is only just graduating from high school and entering college.
>
> I was raised in the Pennsylvania school system from the 1950's through the early 1970's. The curriculum was relevant, competitive, and all extra-curricular subjects were paid for by our taxes.
>
> We had the JFK P.E. program mandatory until graduation; art, music, band, wood and auto shop were given as paid-for electives. Our special Ed teachers were fulltime so the debilitated and disturbed had constant support and camaraderie. No "melting pot" classrooms – gifted w/ gifted, main-stream w/ main-stream, challenged w/ challenged!
>
> Corporal punishment by teachers, staff and parents was a given, but verbal abuse and scapegoats were "out". Tutoring was through student inter-

action and formed a cohesive effort between students and faculty. Even through the race wars, there was more teamwork evident than the common "composite" classrooms of today, and teachers were far less imposed upon.

There were also far fewer administrators and they were pragmatic, innovative and resourceful.

Throughout my daughter's schooling, I was proactive: on the PTA, classroom volunteer, special event volunteer and even a four-year fulltime school employee in the Washington School District.

It was highly frustrating to see teachers struggle with overload on so many levels: too many students from too many "areas;" too many rules from District all focused on "testing;" too many supplies they must supply themselves!; too many parents breathing down their necks instead of working with and for them; too many restrictions to put on students instead of letting them help and grow.

Administrators spend too much time creating "new" methods of teaching [to stay "cutting edge" and "improve"], when there are hundreds of years of proof that the basics of rote learning in reading, writing and arithmetic WORKS!

America was still competitive when these systems were the norm. Countries that have replaced us in the global markets still use them! "HELLO!!!"

Has pride become such an obsession that we can't admit we've wasted time, money and talent for decades with polls and studies that have undermined the entire fabric of our nation's education?

Cut to the chase before it is too late! Our children still have intelligence shining in their eyes. Let's match it with our methods and stop overanalyzing so administrators can keep and do their jobs! Sound a little angry? Aren't you?"

Modern-Day Sugar Tits

In pre-rubber-nipple-pacifier days in America it was common for some mothers to use small pouches of sugar to serve as pacifiers to keep their babies quiet.

With the advent of television and video games many parents began using them as pacifiers for children of all ages. The harm that this has done to several generations of children is incalculable—despite the arguments by some that both of these forms of "entertainment" have educational benefits—an argument that generally was not true because parents did not control or monitor what their kids were watching, and when they did the choice was limited.

Parents should wean their children, especially males, from violence-oriented and otherwise time-wasting video games and television, and provide them with learning games that are designed to attract, challenge, and teach kids at the same time. By 2010 there were dozens of educational video games for parents and kids to choose from. All you need to do is go to Google and put in Educational Video Games, and dozens will come up.

More parents should also take advantage of the programs offered by the Boy Scouts and Girl Scouts, which offer their troops a variety of programs that range from merit badges in geology to science. The success of Scout programs in helping young people learn how to develop knowledge and skills that aid them throughout their lives is apparently not nearly as well known or as appreciated as it should be. Many parents simply don't want to take on the responsibility of enrolling their children and following up on their progress.

Preventing young children, both boys and girls, from being programmed to use physical and emotional violence is a parental responsibility that many parents have obviously failed to fulfill—and it has a dramatic impact on the lives of many students.

Violence on School Campuses

One of the more serious social problems that is rampant in schools is the amount and degree of bullying by both male and female students—bullying that includes both physical actions and the use of digital communication devices.

The problem is serious enough that at a "Bullying Summit" held in 2010 by the U.S. Education Department a committee was formed [!] to come up with measures aimed at getting the practice under control...with a government grant [of course] to finance the effort.

A number of organizations around the country, including the Iowa Pride Network and the National Data Center for School Engagement, were among the first to join in this effort.

A survey by the Josephson Institute of Ethics, a non-profit based in Los Angeles that has been surveying the conduct of teens every two years since 1992 found in its latest survey that 52 percent of the students had hit someone in anger. Even more startling, 37 percent of the boys and 19 percent of the girls said they thought it was OK to hit or threaten a person who had angered them.

Other results of the same survey: 60 percent of the students said they had cheated on tests and 27 percent said they had stolen something from a store. Surprisingly to some, perhaps, 56 percent of the students who said they had cheated attended religious schools, as opposed to 33 percent who attended non-religious schools.

Commenting on the survey results, Sally Kuykendall, professor at Saint Joseph's University in Philadelphia, said that students were being programmed by the preponderance of violence in and depicted by the current culture to believe that violence is an acceptable way of handling problems. She added that media and domestic violence were to blame for much of this mindset.

During the first decade of the 21st century violence at one school in Chicago got so shocking—during the 2009 school year 245 public school students were shot, and 27 of them died—that the school district finally called in a panel of behavioral experts to try to find out which students were most likely to become killers and who their most likely victims.

It turned out that potential *victims* fit a precise category: absent from school up to 40 percent of the time; failing grades; a high rate of disciplinary problems at school [gang activity and drug use], and unlikely to graduate. The school district leaders were advised to assign mentors to the most likely victims, and get them after-school jobs, resulting in a significant fall in the number of shootings and deaths.

Another problem that school administrators and teachers face is sexual abuse on school campuses. Sexual abuse in schools—in some cases beginning in middle school—has become a major problem on some campuses and ranges from cyber bullying to physical assault.

Males are sexual predators by nature, and since the 1960s the popular culture has promoted sexual activity and promiscuity. This has resulted in a significant percentage of boys and girls becoming sexually active by the time they are 14 or 15—which despite all the shock it causes religious-programmed parents and adults in general is a perfectly natural thing for human males and females when they pass puberty.

In a survey of the sexual activities on one high school campus a 15-year-old male interviewee said he had had sexual intercourse with more than 30 girls, all younger than he was, and that he had stopped counting at 30 because it was too much trouble to keep count.

One of the major underlying causes of this phenomenon is the influence of movies, television shows and video games that are based on blatant sexual themes involving preteens and teens as well as adults. The news media also contributes to sexualizing the behavior of young people with its incessant stories and depictions of young movie starlets and other female entertainers engaging in sex-charged dancing, singing and other forms of erotic behavior.

Overall the entertainment industry has been a leader in weakening if not removing virtually all restraints on sexual behavior, not only among the young but among all ages. Religious taboos against sexual behavior outside of wedlock, which were irrational and anti-human in the first place, cannot compete with the culture of the day.

Parents have traditionally been responsible for the moral behavior of their children, and the thought of relinquishing this right to school teachers would no doubt be unthinkable to most of them. But today many parents make no attempt at all to teach their children a morally responsible standard of sexual behavior.

And the efforts of the majority who do accept and attempt to fulfill this obligation have most of their efforts go to waste because of the power of the cultural influences their children are exposed to for several hours a day and often because of the examples set by the parents themselves.

This is another reason why there is a crying need for a universal culture that recognizes the sexual nature of human beings and provides rational and practical solutions. Expecting normal females and males to suppress their sexual urges from puberty until they are in their late teens or early twenties—the period when the urges are the most powerful—is not rational or humane.

Violence-oriented and sex-saturated video games, television shows and movies that are viewed by young boys and girls can surely be blamed for most of the violence on school campuses as well as society in general, despite claims to the contrary by their creators and sellers.

Eliminating or at least reducing the exposure of children and teens to video game depictions of violent behavior—much of it sexual—is the responsibility of parents. The producers will not stop it as long as it is profitable. The developers of these violent games, along with the manufacturers of the devices on which they are shown, employ an army of attorneys to protect their "free-speech" rights to create and sell this culturally insane content.

In 2010 efforts by groups in California to get incredibly violent video games aimed at children banned or at least their sales restricted had reached the Supreme Court, but according to legal experts the efforts seem destined for failure. Even a Supreme Court justice was quoted as saying prior to a ruling that the Jewish-Christian Bible is filled with descriptions of the most heinous violence committed by members of these two faiths, inferring that the idea of banning the Bible is unthinkable.

Another element in the sorrowful example of abusive behavior on school campuses is that other students and sometimes teachers as well often standby and do little or nothing to stop it, no doubt out of fear for their own safety.

The anti-homosexual bias, primarily promoted by religions, that is rampant in the U.S., shows up early in young straight males and has resulted in a series of murders and suicides of students—and is yet another indictment of the irrational and often disastrous effects of religious dogma.

One of the more successful of the efforts of gay groups to combat this insidious influence was a video film created by Seattle-based writer and columnist Dan Savage and his partner of 16 years Terry Miller, published on *YouTube* in September 2010. In the film the two describe their successful and happy lives—an event that inspired other gays to follow suit. Within weeks there were over 700 videos on the Internet featuring mostly gay individuals in all walks of life, including marines, with positive messages for teen gays on how to deal with life-threatening abuse.

The theme of the films is that if gays can live through high school things will get better and they can have a great life. Another service aimed at preventing suicides by gays, lesbians, bisexuals and transgender youths: the Trevor Project, a 24/7 crisis hotline directed by Charles Robbins.

Despite the fact that the extraordinary talents of many homosexuals have led them into entertainment much of the bias against homosexuality is created by the macho side of films and videos.

The Child-Abuse Epidemic

Another aspect of the overall failure of American parents that has an influence on the mental health of pre-and-school-age is the amount and severity of child-abuse occurring in this nation. Childhelp, a non-profit organization, says an average of five children a day die from abuse, and the number who suffer serious mental and physical damage is in the hundreds of thousands.

According to Childhelp child-abuse in the U.S.—mostly committed by fathers, step-fathers, live-in boyfriends and single mothers—results from multiple causes that include alcohol and drug abuse, emotional immaturity, marital disputes, jealousy, and inability to cope with the problems of child-raising.

Many of these children naturally grow up to be maladjusted adults, continuing the problem for the following generation.

Drinking & Drug Problem

Millions of young people in the United States drink alcoholic beverages before they reach the age set by adult politicians—which may be reasonable politically speaking but it is virtually unenforceable.

The abuse of alcohol is extensive and sometimes deadly in both high school and university settings. When someone dies from over-drinking or when there is extensive property damage there are usually calls from some parents, educators and law-makers to set new standards.

But in the United States today both morality and common sense take a backseat to profit-making. The damage done to both students and Americans in general by excessive drinking that is promoted by skillful marketing is incalculable.

This too is a failure of parents to first of all act as responsible adults to use their power as voting citizens to get their elected representatives to reduce the power of the alcohol beverage companies and their advertising cohorts to program young people to drink, while at the same time teaching their children that drinking alcoholic beverages harms their health and can damage or destroy their lives.

In a significant effort to deal with the problems of parenting, Jana Morrison, a Gilbert, Arizona mother of three did something revolutionary about it. She invited 70 other mothers to share with her the best things they knew about bringing up preteens and teens. As a result of the meeting she started a non-profit organization called *Mothers of Teens in 2000* and then following extensive research she designed a class to help mothers navigate their way through the most challenging years in the lives of their children.

After conducting the classes in her own home she began working with parents to start similar classes, called Moms-Props, in their own communities. The topics covered in the classes include peer pressure, attitudes and mouthing off, dating and sex, unresolved anger, seeking purity in today's society, curfews, media dilemmas, technology, setting boundaries and setting limits with teens, parent attitudes, parenting styles and personal issues affecting parenting. The program website is MomPros.com.

Jenny Cook, a mother of five, says: "The material we use never grows old."

The MomsProps organization recommends the following five books: *Parenting Today's Adolescent*, by Dennis and Barbara Rainey; *So You're About to be a Teenager*, by Dennis and Barbara Rainey with Samuel and Rebecca Rainey; *Boundaries with Teens*, by John Sims Townsend; *Interviewing Your Daughter's Date*, by Dennis Rainey; and *Age of Opportunity* by Paul David Tripp.

The Brave New Unmarried World

In the U.S. the whole parenting problem is rapidly taking on a new element that is changing the essence of society. The age-old system of married couples—a man and a woman—is becoming a thing of the past. The institution of marriage is declining as more and more couples simply choose not to get married—a phenomenon made acceptable by entertainers, other celebrities and young cohabiting couples.

The impact this new reality will have on the future is unknown, but there is no doubt that the influence will be fundamental on all levels of social interaction. Among other things the fact that there are no legal ties and no social restraints to keep couples together could lead to even more serial coupling.

By 2010 almost one-third of all children in the country were living in single parent homes—a phenomenon that must have a fundamental influence on the mindset and behavior of children as they are growing up and impact on their values and behavior as adults.

What this means for the future of America can be extrapolated into a number of scenarios, none of which are positive.

Misuse and Abuse of the
Learning Power of Children

The age of computers, the Internet, cell phones and other high-tech devices was a revelation to many parents. They discovered that their young children were far more capable than they were in learning how to use new technology.

While such understanding should have been implicit in the fact that children only several months old can learn how to speak a language and by the age of five or six have accumulated a broad range of knowledge, this insight has long been totally absent from the adult mindset. Among other uninformed positions, renowned educators have traditionally maintained that young kids should not be introduced to a second language until they are in middle school or higher because they would get confused and their overall education would suffer.

The fact is that the learning capacity of children is at its highest peak between the time of their birth and the age of about six. Normal children learn more during this brief period than most of them do during the rest of their lives.

In addition to the basics of education, including reading and writing, children can become fluent in two, three or more languages by the time they are six years old, at which time their learning ability drops off dramatically but they are still able to learn.

The national *United Way* organization has recognized this fundamental factor and offers a "Success by 6" program to parents in the form of school readiness starter kits for preschoolers that feature pictures and word books, with suggestions for parents about activities they can have their children engage in to help them get a jump on learning.

Parents who not aware of and/or do not take advantage of this age-related learning factor and do not provide their children with learning opportunities before they start to school are cheating them and the world at large.

In the present age of technology parents should also make every effort to give their children the opportunity to learn how to operate high-tech devices that are crucial not only to day-to-day living but also to gaining the education that is required to function in today's world, including knowledge of history and other cultures.

Teaching present-day children the difference between reality and illusion is one of the greatest challenges facing parents and teachers, not only because the job is difficult in the first place but particularly now because of the massive exposure of children to images on television, in movies, in video games and in *manga* [mahn-gah] style comics that do not distinguish between reality and illusion.

Both parents and teachers make an effort to help kids recognize and understand the difference between what is real and what is imagined, but this process is generally incomplete even when it continues until the end of formal education.

In today's world several things are essential for the young as well as adults to stay well-founded in reality. These things include knowledge about the source of the things they see and hear and the critical judgment to make the right decisions about them.

The foundation of all higher education should be the ability to view things critically, to question everything—a fact that is virtually ignored by most of today's education system, which is geared to teaching students to accept the opinions and "facts" of others without any standards of measurement or comparison—an approach that works most of the time only where math is concerned.

The process of thinking critically should be a main course in education, starting no later than the age of seven or eight—a concept that is generally neither followed nor acknowledged in the present elementary school system.

The Value of Being Multi-Lingual

Since languages program and control the thinking and behavior of people it is of extreme importance that all
American students, from kindergarten on up, be required to
take and master at least one of the world's top and most
important foreign languages: Mandarin Chinese*, Spanish,
Hindi, Arabic, Japanese, Russian, Portuguese, German,
French, etc.

---

*There are seven [or eight!] major native languages spoken in
China but in 1956 the new Communist leader Mao Tse-Tung
was wise enough to mandate that Mandarin Chinese, the language that prevailed in the Beijing area, would be taught in all
schools as the national language. Prior to this all literate Chinese could communicate with each other through the written
language, since the same ideographic characters, although pronounced differently, were used to write all of the so-called
Chinese dialects. But the linguistic-cultural differences that had
historically separated the Chinese were a source of serious
political, social and economic problems. By the 1970s all of the
young people of China had learned the newly mandated national
language, and for the first time in the history of this huge land-
mass the next generation of the linguistic and ethic groups of
China was able to communicate with each other verbally.

By 2011 there had been a remarkable turnaround
throughout the United States in the number of schools
offering classes in foreign languages. In my state of Arizona—previously very backward in that regard—several
school districts were offering classes in Mandarin Chinese.
The first Arizona school to begin teaching Chinese has the
intriguing name of Whispering Wind Elementary School—
and indication that the school had a different perspective of
the world to begin with.

Located in the Paradise Valley Unified School District,
this school established a tie-up with Qiyi [Chee-yee]

Primary School in Beijing, China and has been teaching Chinese since 2008.

The U.S. Foreign Service and Defense Language Institutes rank languages according to the time it takes to become fluent in them. Chinese is ranked in Category 4, meaning it takes a minimum of 44 weeks [1,100 class hours] for students to understand and speak the language fairly well. This comes out as five hours a day, 25 hours a week.

Spanish and Portuguese, Category 1 languages, are listed as requiring only 24 weeks [600 hours] of study. I don't have the ranking for Japanese, but it is probably a Category 3 because it is not tonal, like Chinese. Say a word in the wrong tone in Chinese and you can be in serious trouble. Most other languages are in Categories that range from 2 to 4.

What the above organizations do not mention is that full fluency in a language for most people requires extensive study and practice outside of school hours. To absorb the subtle nuances and uses of key words in languages also requires immersion *within* the culture of the language, not just classroom learning.

Parents in school districts that do not offer students multiple choices in the study of foreign languages should demand that these classed be offered, and make sure that their children enroll in at least one of them, beginning in kindergarten and continuing each year through K-12.

It is also vitally important that the English language be designated by law as the national language of the country in order to avoid the kind of problems that divide and degrade societies in which there is more than one mother language. The steps taken to accommodate Spanish-speaking residents of the U.S. may seem the right thing to do, but that is a shortsighted solution that will come back to haunt the country if it is continued.

Languages, Not Things,
Transmit Culture

What most of mankind, educators in particular, has missed over the millennia has been the relationship between language and culture. Languages are, in fact, the repository as well as the transmitter of cultures. Languages are the essence, the tone, the flavor and the spirit of cultures, and serve as doorways to understanding them.

Most people still today mistakenly regard the arts, crafts and other things of individual societies as their "culture." Arts, crafts and other things reflect culture but they do not create it and they do not transmit it. You can view and collect Chinese artifacts or Eskimo artifacts all your life and you will not become conversant with the cultures that created them.

The influence that indigenous languages have on the values, attitudes and behavior of people is fundamental, and is one of the primary reasons why the present-day world is in a constant state of turmoil. We cannot communicate fully and effectively across the cultural barriers inherent in languages.

It is fairly simple to interpret or translate technical subjects from one language into another, but translating cultural attitudes and values into another language ranges from difficult to impossible. The translations may be perfectly correct as far as the words are concerned, but they seldom if ever include all of the cultural nuances that are bound up in the words and are the essence of the original language.

This results in people talking at each other instead of to each other—and generally neither side understands why they are seldom if ever in perfect agreement with each other… why they cannot get along.

It takes no great intellect or scholarship to recognize that the French think and behave differently from all other people, sometimes in subtle ways and other times in ways that are very conspicuous.

This difference applies to all people who are separated from others by language, and because typical Americans are the least sensitive to these cultural differences they often find themselves criticized and attacked by foreigners seemingly without cause—not to mention the mistakes they typically make in interacting with people of other cultures.

There are obviously several factors in the creation of languages that make them unique, and these cultural-laden factors are not the result of conscious planning. They evolve naturally from a variety of influences that fashion and control the life-styles of the people involved.

Again, any attempt to truly understand the character and personality of Chinese Germans, Japanese, Koreans, Mexicans or any other group of people—to put yourself in their shoes, as the saying goes—must include a deep knowledge of the cultural essences of their languages, and this is a challenge facing mankind that cannot be easily or quickly resolved.

Universal translators are not the solution. *Star Trek*-type universal translators were introduced in China and Japan in the first decade of this century. But they translate only the technical and objective meaning of the words; not the subjective meanings; not the cultural nuances. They simply cannot transmit or communicate feelings. That is something that comes only with language learning combined with cultural immersion, and is something I have written about extensively in a series of "cultural code word" books on China, Japan, Korea and Mexico.

In today's world, and more so in the future, knowledge of the cultures of other countries is an absolute prerequisite for understanding and cooperation—and is a lesson that American leaders have not yet fully learned.

Learning Lessons
From a Success Guru

One of the belated improvements in the concept of teaching children adopted by some schools in 2010 was incorporating proven success strategies into the education system based on the book *The 7 Habits of Highly Effective People* written by Stephen Covey, which had sold over 15 million copies, mostly to businesspeople. Covey then published *The Leader in Me: How Schools and Parents around the World are Inspiring Greatness, One Child at a Time.*

Covey's son, Sean, who writes about the same subject, later published an illustrated version of his father's book called *The 7 Habits of Happy Kids.*

As reported by journalist Ray Parker in *The Arizona Republic*, among the first pioneers in adopting the success and learning principles popularized by Stephen Covey's books were Frank Elementary School in Guadalupe, Arizona and Kyrene de los Cerritos Elementary School in Awatukee Foothills, Arizona, which launched its *The Leader in Me* program under the direction of Principal Darcy DiCosmo. The 7 habits in the program:

Habit 1 - Be proactive. [You are in charge]

Habit 2 - Begin with the End in Mind [Have a plan]

Habit 3 - Put First Things First [Work first, then play]

Habit 4 - Think Win-Win [So that everyone can win]

Habit 5 - Seek First to Understand Then to be Understood. Listen before you speak]

Habit 6 - Synergize [Work with others to get the best Results]

Habit 7 - Sharpen the Saw [Learn to live in balance; in harmony]

Andi Fourlis, assistant superintendent of teaching and learning in the Scottsdale, Arizona Unified School District, was another pioneer in using the 7 Habits concepts. She came up with her own version of Covey's rules, adding that students are far more likely to be successful when their parents model and teach them the following seven rules:

Rule 1 - Develop your organization skills: how to organize materials; how to use a calendar to write down assignment due dates and long-term projects; how to set realistic goals.

Rule 2 - Learn time-management: how to break up projects into chunks of time; how to allocate enough time to complete tasks; how to balance time to include school and family expectations with social activities.

Rule 3 - Celebrate success along the way: reward yourself as you accomplish tasks.

Rule 4 - Ask for help: learn how you learn best. If you have trouble learning something, ask to be taught in a way that makes sense to you. Know when to ask for clarification and get feedback. Make corrections on assignments.

Rule 5 - Be a good listener.

Rule 6 - Be honest; don't cheat.

Rule 7 - Be healthy. Take care of yourself emotionally and physically; make good decisions; surround yourself with people who make good choices.

Ancient Wisdom: Stilling the Mind

Wise parents learned long ago that teaching children how to be quiet—to neither speak nor move for short periods of time—had beneficial effects that served them throughout their lives.

In India, China, Korea and Japan this ancient wisdom was incorporated into the common culture and both institutionalized and ritualized as meditation—one of the primary practices in Zen Buddhism. Very early it was discovered that meditating regularly for extended periods results in dramatically increasing the individual's ability to think calmly and clearly, and eventually to help recognize the different between what is illusion and what is real.

I recommend that all schools in the American educational system, from kindergarten through university, begin the first class each morning with a minimum of five minutes of meditation.

Too many Americans dismiss the concept of meditation as mystical nonsense because it originated in Asia. However, it has been practiced for thousands of years by millions of people and has proven to have measureable physical and psychological benefits.

The growth of meditation in its earliest modern form is attributed to an Indian Buddhist monk name Daruma who lived during the 5th and 6th centuries A.D. He is also credited with having introduced the practice into China, where it came to be known as Ch'an Buddhism [ch'an translates as meditation].

In the early 1200s a Japanese Buddhist priest named Dōgen spent several years in China, during which he was introduced to Ch'an Buddhism. He returned to Kamakura,

Japan [then the Shogunate capital of the country] in 1227, where he incorporated meditation into his services and it soon became known as Zen Buddhism [Zen being the Japanese pronunciation of Ch'an]. Over the centuries a number of "Zen schools" were formed by other Japanese Buddhist monks, and they have continued to flourish.

In the 1960s and early 70s a new form of Zen meditation known as Transcendental Meditation [TM] was introduced into the United States by an Indian Hindu priest named Mahesh Brasad Warma.

At the beginning of his career Mahesh studied under a famous *Guru Dev* [Devine Teacher] named Saraswart, who had spent 40 years as a recluse in the Himalayas striving to achieve perfect enlightenment through direct intuition by meditating. Mahesh himself then spent three years in a cave, changed his name to Maharishi [Great Sage], and then assumed the mantle of his old teacher who had advised him to introduce Zen Buddhism to Americans.

In 1958 Maharishi established the Spiritual Regeneration Movement in Madras. His stated aim was nothing less than the spiritual regeneration of all mankind.

Through the influence of one Ravi Shankhat, Maharishi attracted the attention of the Beatles [yes, the Beatles who had already achieved musical immortality!]. The Beatles quickly took up the practice of TM, sang its praises, and got millions of dollars worth of publicity around the world for the Great Sage.

But the interest of the Beatles soon waned, resulting in Maharishi modifying his teaching for Western audiences and using a 1970s scientific research report that supported his claims of the physical and psychological benefits of TM as a springboard to go international.

Maharishi trained several thousand teachers, sponsored the formation of a TM world organization, established thousands of teaching centers, and within a year the practice of TM had become a world-wide phenomenon.

The modified version of TM had no religious content whatsoever, and was therefore acceptable to everyone.

I am a strong advocate of introducing a further modified form of TM into the American education system, making it mandatory that the first class of the day begin with a 5-minute simplified 4-step process of meditation, beginning with precise instructions by the teachers repeated daily until the students get it.

Step 1: Students are instructed to sit at their desks motionless and perfectly quiet.

Step 2: Students are instructed to breathe slowly and deeply seven times, from the abdomen, exhaling quietly.

Step 3: Students are instructed to relax all of their muscle groups beginning with the clinched fists and proceeding all the way down to the feet by silently addressing each of these parts.

Step 4: Teachers then instruct the students, in the words of Dr. Oz of TV fame, to send their minds on a journey to a beautiful and soothing place for the rest of the 5-minute period...a practice that by itself will gradually have a positive effect on their attitudes and behavior for the rest of the school day, and eventually on their lives in general.

The calming effect of five minutes of quiet repose by stilling the body and the mind will by itself bring a new and beneficial factor into the education scenario. To get more beneficial effects from meditation at-home sessions should be at least 15 minutes—the timeframe recommended by TM masters.

Again, there are no religious connotations involved in transcendental meditating. It is a natural physical process that is based on two things: deep measured breathing and the repetition of a mantra or key word that resonates with the human brain, which together have an immediate impact on the body, removing stress and creating a link with the invisible energy of the cosmos.

Religious advocates should remind themselves that somewhere in the Bible itself it says "Be still and know thy self!"—first said centuries earlier by Chinese philosopher Lao Tzu (604-531 B.C.) who phrased it this way: "Man was made to sit quietly and find the truth within."

TEACHER FAILURES
& FIXES

Obstacles Teachers Face

If teachers are not respected and students are not cared for, confusion will rise no matter how clever people are—Lao Tzu, Chinese philosopher (604-531 B.C.]

Historically, teaching was an honored profession. The parents of children lucky enough to be allowed to send their children to school—and had schools for them to go to—understood the role that teachers played in the lives of their children and in the state of their society from one generation to the next.

But by the last two decades of the 20th century the recognition of the importance of education and the status of teachers in the United States, particularly up to K-12, had degenerated to the point that they were a national disgrace.

The obstacles that teachers have to deal with today on a daily basis—some because of the system and others because of the character and behavior of their students—can lead to burnout, especially for teachers who are not totally committed to the profession.

These obstacles include bureaucratic administrative duties that take up a significant proportion of the teachers' day; so many students in a class that teachers cannot give individual attention to most of them; classes that are made up of fast learners; slow learners and other students who don't even try to learn; and students who deliberately and repeatedly create distractions.

Beginning in the mid-1900s, when the teaching profession in the United States still attracted some of the best and the brightest, teachers both good and bad began to be subjected to circumstances that made their job a daily grind instead of a pleasure. Sustaining their passion for teaching was often impossible.

Still today many teachers who never had the necessary passion or lost it choose to stay in the profession, but they do little more than go through the motions... ensuring that another generation of students will not get the full benefit of a good education.

The formation of teachers' unions was obviously an attempt to improve the status and security of teachers and to improve teaching standards. At first, as with other labor unions, the unions were successful in providing more security for teachers and in the early years both the status and the standards of teachers went up. But eventually the bureaucracy syndrome got the upper hand, and maintaining union membership and teacher security became more important than teaching standards.

This cultural failure of the unions results in many of those who do go into the teaching profession, and stay in the profession, lacking both the level of knowledge and experience that is necessary to meet today's demands, as well as the passion that is an essential attribute for a good teacher.

Again, this is often not the fault of the teacher concerned. It is the system and the whole cultural environment that now pervades American society. These cultural failures keep talented people from joining the teaching profession and drive others away.

There is another more insidious cultural failure that has usurped control of what goes into the textbooks that teachers are required to use.

The Textbook Police

One of the most controversial aspects of the American education system involves the editing that occurs in the content textbooks—a scandalous situation that impacts on the core of traditional American culture. Groups of people with powerful agendas that range from religion and homosexuality to race basically control what is printed or not printed in textbooks, resulting in bias, stereotyping, misinformation, political correctness and more being rampant throughout the textbook publishing industry.

A book entitled *The Language Police: How Pressure Groups Restrict what Students Learn*, by noted education historian Diane Ravitch, details this startling scandal. A description of the book states that efforts in the 1960s and 1970s to achieve fairness and a balanced perspective in the nation's textbooks and in standardized exams was necessary and commendable, but "something went terribly wrong."

Ravitch, who is the author of six other books on education and served as Assistant Secretary of Education from 1991 to 1993, explains what went wrong in her informative and frightening book. She describes in copious detail how pressure groups from the political right and left have wrested control of the language and content of textbooks and standardized exams, often at the expense of the truth, literary quality, and education in general.

Ravitich ends her book with three suggestions of how to counter this disturbing tendency. Sadly, however, in the face of the overwhelming tide of misinformation that has already been entrenched in the system, her suggestions provide cold comfort.

In its review of *The Language Police*, the book industry's *Publishers Weekly*, notes Ravitch's argument that textbook publishers are guilty of self-censorship and goes on to say that her polemical analysis of the anti-bias and sensitivity guidelines that govern much of today's edu-

128

cational publishing shows how publishers are squeezed by pressure from groups on the right (which object to depictions of disobedience, family conflict, sexuality, evolution and the supernatural) and the left (which "corrects" for the racism and sexism of older textbooks by urging stringent controls on language and images to weed out possibly offensive stereotypes)—and that most publishers have quietly adopted both sets of suggestions.

There is no shortage of colorful examples in Ravitch's book: a scientific passage about owls was rejected from a standardized test because the birds are taboo for Navajos; one set of stereo-type guidelines urges writers to avoid depicting "children as healthy bundles of energy;" editors of a science textbook rejected a sentence about fossil fuels being the primary cause of global warming because it would never be adopted in Texas. Readers will likely disagree about whether anti-bias guidelines do more harm than good, but Ravitch's detailed, concise, impassioned argument raises crucial questions for parents and educators.

Fixing all of the problems besetting teachers is a formidable task and may be impossible in the present culture. But sincere efforts are being made by a growing number of fine, dedicated teachers and organizations and some of the results show.

Cathy Ballman, a dedicated teacher at Phoenix, Arizona's South Mountain High School, was one of the many individuals attempting to make a difference. She blames politicians, not teachers and not students, for most of the problems besetting the education system, and dares them to come to her classroom and meet her students.

Her position is that it is easy for legislators who have never been in a classroom to criticize from the sidelines and make decisions that do more harm than good; that before they open their mouths they should go to the schools in their districts, talk to teachers, listen to what they need and want for their students.

As already noted, one of the greatest obstacles facing teachers is not self-made or made by administrators or politicians. It is made by parents who do not, for whatever reason, prepare their children for the education process.

Part of this failure is a combination of parental ignorance, irresponsibility and slothfulness. Another part has to do with the psychological mindset of the children—some of which is induced by the culture and some of which is apparently the result of them having been fed and otherwise absorbed chemicals that interfere with rational thinking and behavior.

Research published in 2010 revealed that the brains and bodies of not only children but fetuses in their mothers' wombs were impregnated with chemicals from the air the mothers breathed and the food they ate.

Corruption of the English Language!

Given the fundamental role that language plays in human interaction, especially when dealing with foreign cultures, it is galling to note that the English language itself is another victim of the dysfunctional parental and education systems and the negative influence of the entertainment industries in the United States and elsewhere.

Two simple but very conspicuous examples of the debasement of the language are the widespread use of "went missing" in place of "disappeared" by the news media, and the growing habit of people to arbitrarily and indiscriminately add the word "like" to almost everything they say that is more than three or four words long…often making them sound like they are suffering from some kind of brain disorder.

Parents, teachers and older friends and relatives are at fault if they do not correct children and kids when they use such cock-eyed English as "I like called my friend," "I am like never going to get this done!"

There are just five rules for good speech and good writing: simplicity, clarity, continuity, integrity and euphony. But these rules are broken more often than not by educators as well as students.

If it is left up to the creators of "popular culture" to debase the language as they see fit, the communications gap between the post-1960 generations and the "old ones" will become even more formidable than what it is today.

Another language factor that parents, teachers, administrators and politicians should keep in mind are the cultural conflicts that naturally arise in societies in which more than one language is spoken by a large number of people.

As already noted, languages create and sustain cultures, and when two are more exist in the same society the divisions in values and behavior can range from slight to profound, and in the latter case have serious detrimental results.

Extreme examples of this situation exist in Asia, in Africa and elsewhere and should make the dangers obvious to everyone, but as is the case in so much of human behavior the problem is so basic it often goes unnoticed or is ignored—especially by mainstream Americans.

ADMINISTRATOR FAILURES & FIXES

Running School Districts

Managing a school district is one of the most demanding jobs in the country. It is not and never has been the purview of an educator. It is a multi-faceted challenge that requires a high level of business acumen, financial smarts, political finesse and people skills. A weakness in any of these areas can act like a cancer or virus that degrades the overall quality of management.

After Dr. Gary T. Catalani became superintendent of the Scottsdale Unified School District in Arizona he used an approach to managing the education process that precisely reflected the above attributes. His process—arrived at by a panel of faculty, staff, administration personnel and parents—consisted of a strategic action plan that incorporated belief and value statements, a mission statement, a vision statement, and high priority goals like taking advantage of the latest information technology for distance-learning programs

All schools should have such statements and action plans and have them prominently displayed in class-rooms, in hall-ways and in offices—and made available to all parents of students in the district as well as to local businesses that should support public schools.

School principals should also have similar skills in addition to empathy and understanding of the problems of teaching. Principals should be evaluated annually by the teachers in their schools, and if a significant proportion of the teachers charge their principals with attitudes and behavior that is not in keeping with the responsibilities of the job the district superintendent should fire them...not just move them to some other school.

In school districts that have governing boards the qualifications of the board candidates should be equally demanding, and voters who go to the polls without knowing who they are and what they stand for are at fault.

New Leaders for New Schools

In 2000 a team of young "social entrepreneurs" founded an organization called *New Leaders for New Schools*. In the words of the founders, it attracts, prepares, and supports outstanding individuals to become the next generation of school leaders in response to the immense need for exceptional principals in our nation's urban public schools.

The organization was first conceived by five business and education graduate students. Throughout the planning and design phase, the team drew upon extensive interviews with school leaders and district superintendents, their own experiences as classroom teachers and leaders, and the most current thinking in education and policy.

The result was a unique model which trains aspiring school leaders in instructional, transformational, and organizational leadership through combining coursework and practical application.

Continuing in the words of the founders, more than a principal training program, New Leaders for New Schools is a national movement of leaders with an unwavering commitment to ensure that every student achieves academic excellence.

New Leaders for New Schools grew rapidly. By 2001 it had trained 13 leaders in New York City and Chicago. By 2008 the total number of New Leaders had grown to over 550.

New Leaders for New Schools has also had a catalytic impact on the public education system. After introducing the New City Competition in 2002 there has been increasing demand from districts for New Leaders principals and programs. By 2010 its New York City partners had been joined by 20-plus other cities that had adopted elements of the New Leaders for New Schools' model in developing their own principal training programs, and this number has continued growing.

The stated mission of *New Leaders for New Schools* is to make forward progression and true transformation of public education the next civil rights movement. The organization is at the forefront of this movement, breaking new ground with dramatic improvements in urban school performance, elevating urban student achievement beyond ordinary to extraordinary. Stellar academic success achieved by New Leaders principals in some of America's major urban centers is clear evidence that children from all communities can achieve at the highest levels.

These leaders are described as influential agents of change who impact not only on students and schools but on entire communities, producing high school graduates well prepared for college, careers, and beyond.

The founders of *New Leaders for New Schools* add: "It is our mission to ensure high academic achievement for every student by attracting and preparing outstanding leaders and supporting the performance of the urban public schools they lead at scale." The organization lists its core beliefs as:

1. Every student can achieve at high levels.

2. All adults must take personal responsibility for student learning and achievement.

3. Great schools are led by great leaders.

4. With access to outstanding public education, all students can unlock their fullest potential in the classroom and in life.

5. Delivering high-quality public education to all students is critical to a just society.

Rules Parents Should Teach Their Children

Virginia McElyea, Superintendent of the Deer Valley United School District in Arizona, recommends that parents make a serious effort to instill the following seven habits in their children to ensure that they become effective students:

Rule 1 - Take responsibility for your own ideas and actions.

Rule 2 - Set challenging goals for your learning and your personal development. Begin with the end in mind so that you can monitor your progress and make adjustments as needed.

Rule 3 - Communicate effectively with your parents, teachers, classmates and the other adults in our life. Listen actively to the words spoken, the body language and what is not said. Ask questions for clarification and understanding. Express your thoughts with clarity.

Rule 4 - Respect the diversity in people, cultures and ideas.

Rule 5 - Work collaboratively with others on assignments, tasks and service projects. Learn to lead, to follow and to be an effective team member.

Rule 6 - Manage your time wisely. Prioritize your work and complete the most important things first.

Rule 7 - Work hard and persist in completing tasks to accomplish your goals.

Achieving or even attempting to achieve these goals requires a level of intellectual and emotional maturity that is generally not present in children under the age of seven of eight, but parents should begin the process of teaching these concepts and practices to their children from the age of five or six.

Again, the learning ability of normal children up to the age of six or seven is incredible, and with intelligent and thoughtful parental guidance they can achieve levels of knowledge and responsibility that is astounding in the present-day culture of mediocrity.

PART II
Living in today's World

America's present-day public education system obviously contains the seeds for its own destruction, and despite its inefficiencies and those who resist change, change is coming. And even at this time of anguish all is not gloom and doom in education. Throughout the United States there are hundreds of thousands of high school and university students who are wonderful examples of intelligence, diligence, goodwill and good works.

New technology that has obvious powerful benefits, and is more effective in changing age-old beliefs, customs and entrenched practices of people than anything else, is changing the nature of education, and it goes without saying it will totally transform the system before the middle of this century.

In all states throughout the country the growth of online education [also known as distance learning] is going forward with increasing speed. This nationwide trend has reached self-sustaining momentum, and will speed up until it blankets the country. New technologies in classrooms are adding enormously to the effectiveness of teachers and teaching.

In the meantime, more programs are needed to rescue the hundreds of thousands of students and young adults who have been left behind by failings that have plagued the public education system since its inception.

There is no way the present official education system can remedy this situation quickly, but there are partial answers to the problem. One such approach is a nationwide

Volunteer Literacy Program patterned on the concept created and initiated by the Navajo Elementary School in the Scottsdale, Arizona United School District.

When neurosurgeon Dr. Fred Christensen retired he volunteered to tutor failing students in his specialties, math and science, at a nearby school. The principal soon asked him to teach reading instead, which was far more critical.

This quickly morphed into the Navajo Volunteer Literacy Program, under the auspices of the school's Hon Kachina Council, consisting of 75 volunteers who were professionals in a number of fields [engineers, nurses, speech therapists, clinical psychologists, educators, etc.]. The volunteers signed up to teach for two hours one day a week in one-on-one sessions that last for 25 minutes.

All of the volunteers underwent training programs designed to teach *them* how to teach children before they could participate in the program, which went on to become immensely successful.

Dr. Christensen, who was 70 when he retired and began a second career as a volunteer teacher, advises all professionals who are on the verge of retiring or already retired to consider joining or creating a volunteer teaching group in their school districts.

This could bring hundreds of thousands of exceptional "teachers' aides" into the education system without adding to the cost—not to mention the satisfaction that the volunteers get from helping to resolve one of the most critical problems facing Americans.

Volunteering to help at schools is not new, of course. But this generation of older Americans might consider the fact that in the traditional culture of Native American Indians all older people automatically became mentors to the younger generations—a natural process that existed in all pre-Industrial Age cultures.

This age-old custom should be reintroduced into American culture on a formal, national basis, with organizations like local chambers of commerce supporting them in co-operation with local school districts.

Joining the 21st Century

In some school districts the transformation from lectures and blackboards to integrating teaching with the technology of the day has moved forward with amazing speed. At the close of the first decade of the 21st century Daniel J. Quigley, an *Independent Newspapers* journalist quoted Andi Fourlist, assistant superintendent for teaching and learning in the Scottsdale Unified District [SUSD] in Scottsdale, Arizona and a pioneer in this movement as noting that the challenge facing educators today is to integrate what students do in their spare time with the teaching curriculum.

Fourlis said that the explosion of technologies since 1990 had turned young people into visual learners who feed off of small bits of information and that this transformation had occurred so fast that the lesson plans of many schools could not keep up with it.

One of the earliest pioneer teachers in this pursuit of efficiency and excellence was Jen MacColl, freshman biology teacher at Chaparral High School in Scottsdale. She went from the old-fashioned blackboard to a *SMART Board*—the 21st century version of the ancient chalk board—that had an overhead projector, a video player and a computer...all in one unit. And instead of having to speak loudly and continuously repeat herself she had a Lavalier microphone hanging around her neck that floated her voice clearly throughout the room no matter which way she was facing of what she was doing.

Ms. MacColl did not have to struggle to come up with content for use on her *SMART Board*. That was provided by Discovery Education, a division of Discovery Communications, best known for its Discovery, Science and

Animal Planet channels available throughout the U.S. on cable TV.

SUSD contracted with Discovery Communications to access its *Discovery Education Streaming Plus*, which offers more than 150,000 clips of video, audio, photos and articles for teachers to use on their *SMART Boards* and incorporate into their curriculum in the appropriate content area and grade level.

Brad Hagarman, sales manager for Discovery Education, said that SUSD and other school districts had recognized that today's students learn in different ways and interact with content differently than previous generations, and that being able to engage students with digital content is essential.

However, even with all of the advantages of high-tech devices and the Internet there is still a vital role for human teachers to play in shaping the character, ambitions and skills of the young, particularly in their ability to understand the mindset and behavior of people from other cultures and to interact with them in positive and effective ways.

Another area that has long been a fundamental factor in the education of each generation but has been short-changed since the mid-1900s is the role that mechanical and technical skills play in the functioning of society. In earlier times these skills were taught to individuals through the master-apprentice approach—young boys and girls learned from their parents or other adults how to perform essential tasks.

This master-apprentice approach to passing skills on from one generation to the next has virtually disappeared in the increasingly urbanized America, and has not been sufficiently replaced by such training in public schools or in private tech schools.

There are, however, a growing number of new approaches involving various kinds companies that should be adopted on a much larger scale. A good example of this is provided by General Dynamics, which provides internships for students interested in careers as engineers.

Companies providing internships is, of course, common, but General Dynamics seems to have been the first company to team students with their own engineers on real jobs in real time. General Dynamics began its engineer intern program by utilizing its connection with Boys & Girls Clubs to identify and recruit students for its eCrew program.

A spokesperson for the program said that despite recruiting engineering graduates from colleges nationwide there are not enough of them to replace the veteran engineers who retired each year.

On the international scene basic cultural differences continue to plague mankind, and progress in reducing much less eliminating them is still in its infancy.

Some people believe that *Star Trek*-type universal translators, introduced in Japan and China during the first decade of the 20th century, will go a long way toward solving most of the international communication and cooperation problems plaguing the United States. But as already mentioned they translate only the technical and objective meanings of the words; not the subjective meanings; not the cultural nuances. They cannot transmit or communicate feelings.

By the first decade of the 21st century technology that could provide real-time translations in different languages was becoming commonplace in Asia. Other software and mobile devices that were as thin and as light as paper and responded to the movement of the eyes were also appearing annually.

This ongoing development will have an increasingly positive effect on communication between societies on all levels—political, economic and social—but it will not eliminate the need for cultural literacy—an area that has traditionally been missing from most of world's education systems and still today is only in its infancy.

The first nations to understand and take steps to remedy this particular educational failing were China, South Korea and India, all of which in 2010 mandated that programs for teaching the cultures of the world's leading economic nations be integrated into their education systems.

It is vital that all people in all cultures and societies be brought into the 21st century as rapidly as possible, and the means to do that are now available. All that is needed is the goodwill and the will. One of the epochal changes that is already well underway is the use of robots.

The Age of Robots!

Sophisticated robotic devices were standard in many manufacturing operations by the 1980s. The use of such devices in all areas of manufacturing, warehousing and distribution has continued to grow, and by 2010 in Japan and elsewhere humanized robots were in use in many service industries.

It takes no great intellect to realize that robotic devices and humanized robots are going to replace a significant proportion of all manual labor tasks as well as many of the tasks in virtually all other fields of endeavor, including health care and surgery, within this century. Coming to terms with this new world will be one of the most fundamental cultural and industrial challenges mankind has ever faced.

The future of robotic devices in the health care industry was abundantly clear by 2011 when over 1,000 American hospitals were using the da Vinci robot to perform prostate cancer removal and other delicate operations…and the use of the da Vinci robot alone was growing worldwide.

Pioneered and promoted by India-born Dr. Mani Menon, director of the Vattikuti Urology Institute at Henry Ford, the da Vinci robot is a harbinger of things to come.

The integration of high-tech devices into education systems in the U.S. were also well underway by the end of the first decade of the 21st century, and their number and sophistication will continue to increase with each passing year. The question is: how far will they go in replacing live teachers.

The programming of robots to have the most desirable qualities of human beings has advanced so rapidly that they are becoming and will be much smarter than humans, capable of interacting with humans on an extraordinary level.

Fans of the prescient *Next Generation* television and film series *Star Trek* [which began in 1987] have only to consider the robot *Lt. Commander Data* to clearly see where robotics are going. *Data* is smarter, stronger and faster than any human being ever could be, never needs rest, never needs sleep, can absorb huge amounts of new information in milliseconds, never forgets anything, and doesn't deteriorate with age.

By 2010 in Japan robots were already being used as assistant nurses, assistant doctors, maids, tour guides, information specialists, product spokesmen, guards, and more. There is virtually no end to what robots can be programmed to do now, and with each passing year they will be able to do more and do it better.

The question is: how will humanity handle the future *Datas*. Will they all be programmed to be tolerant and kind and protective of human beings and do only good things?

Given the history of humanity the answer to this question is not necessarily "Yes." It is very likely that some of the engineers who create or obtain and program the first *Datas* will be influenced by their culture, their race, their tribal affiliations, their religions and so on—a frightening thought.

But long before the evolution of robots reaches the *Data* stage they will be used for destructive purposes. In fact, they already are. Drone planes carrying bombs, which have been a weapon of war since the early 21st century, were a species of robots.

Writer Bill Christensen noted in 2006 that Japan's Ministry of Economy, Trade and Industry was working on a new set of safety guidelines for next-generation robots. Their set of regulations constituted the first attempt at a formal version of the first of writer Isaac Asimov's science-fictional *Laws of Robotics*, or at least the portion that states that humans shall not be harmed by robots.

The first law of robotics, as set forth in 1940 by Asimov, states: *A robot may not injure a human being, or, through inaction, allow a human being to come to harm.*

Christensen goes on to note that Japan's ministry guidelines require manufacturers to install a sufficient number of sensors to keep robots from running into people and hurting them. Emergency shut-off buttons are also required.

At that time the Japanese were particularly concerned about this problem due to their accelerating efforts to create robots to address the labor shortage in the elder care industry.

Made-in-Japan robots are unlikely to become a threat to mankind, but that will not necessarily hold true for all other countries. It is easy to image future wars being fought by robots, just like in the film series *Star Wars*.

Of course, the greatest danger that might come from highly intelligent robots—also already suggested by science fiction movies—is that they would become self-aware and decide to make humans their servants—or worse.

The only hope for humanity is that the superior intelligence of robots—and no human history baggage in their brain chips—would result in them becoming gods instead of devils. One of Japan's top robotics experts, Dr. Hiroshi Ishiguro, who has designed and built a robot based on his appearance as well as his mindset and behavior says that human-like robots are mirrors that reflects human beings and should be treated as such—a very sobering thought.

In the meantime, and on a brighter side, one of the most obvious uses of smart robots at this time in history is as teachers. Just image: no pay; no time off; no emotional meltdowns; no incompetence; no unions!

Technology as God!

Given all the negative influences in the cultures of the world the only salvation for humanity may be technology—which by itself is rapidly changing all of the world's cultures. In the long run, even without forward thinking and forward-acting leaders, the world's cultures will become more and more rational, and more and more democratic because of the universal, objective, unemotional, impersonal, influence of technology.

But given the fact that primitive religions and authoritarian political forms still have at least a partial death-grip on the majority of mankind, these transformations could take generations because educators and political leaders will not take the heroic steps necessary to change today's morality and today's policies…even if they *want* it to happen!

And, of course, there are many leaders who are dead-set against freedom and against a humane morality for the people they rule over.

As a result, most people may continue to be oppressed and prevented from achieving their full potential for generations to come…unless these changes are aggressively promoted by huge numbers of people blogging the world's bureaucrats and leaders in business, in politics and in religions with criticism and advice! And even more importantly, by simply refusing to go along with stupid, insane policies and the people who promote them!

Of course, there are thousands of things one can point to in the U.S. and elsewhere that are encouraging. I saw in a recent news article that American entrepreneurs have established etiquette schools to teach young kids basic good manners, something that parents used to do in their homes.

But how many schools that teach manners and the accompanying morality do you think it will take and how long will it take to counter all of the course behavior and lack of ethics that are being programmed into the minds of millions of children and young people seven days and nights a week by the so-called entertainment industries?

Of course, the majority of people everywhere are sickened by all of these cultural failures. But survival, power and profit-making...not moral behavior...are the overwhelming goals of most leaders in politics and business. And as already said, there is no way that the weak, divided and often irrational spiritual-based moralities of today are going to change that!

We therefore need to teach and follow a philosophy of living and working that is based on common sense, on the fragile nature of the Earth, on the real physical, emotional, intellectual, spiritual and philosophical needs of human beings.

Of course, there are people already espousing these philosophies but with so little impact that contemplating the future is frightening. Despite the misuse and abuse of the Internet by hate mongers, pornographers and radical religious zealots, this new technology also makes it possible for the average person to make his or her voice heard on a large scale for the first time in the history of mankind.

Ordinary people can now vote and express themselves online at any time on very important issues of the day! If enough rational, educated, morally enlightened people will bring more and more pressure against leaders in every field to force them to give up their self-serving ways—or force them out of positions of authority and let a new breed of people have a go at it—the ancient religious promise of peace on earth might be achieved.

Two of the more obvious things that we in the United States are now talking about—and could do if we had the will—is to reintroduce discipline and a reality-based future-oriented curriculum into the educational system, and to boycott purveyors of obscene, immoral and harmful ideas and behavior instead of rewarding them with fame and great wealth.

Just as obviously, the First Amendment of the Constitution should be amended to prohibit its abuse by the so-called entertainment industries—and the so-called news media as well. In addition to being morally inexcusable, the present system is socially insane.

One of the fundamental imperatives in bringing humanity into the new world of the 21st century within a universal culture is the need for a higher level of wisdom combined with better training systems that are integrated into the culture. This wisdom has existed for millennia and there have been some examples of education and training systems that created outstanding people.

However, humans have screwed up and misused far simpler technology than what is now appearing in the world of robotics, which pales with what will appear just in the next few decades. Without a dramatic overhaul of world cultures, based on a 21st century education system, technology will no doubt continue to be both God and Satan.

Why Humanity Needs
A New Cultural Paradigm

Humanity is in dire need of a new cultural paradigm—one that includes parenting, teaching, economics, politics, entertainment and guidelines for sexual behavior that recognizes and accounts for the built-in sexuality—the real sexual needs—of males and females. This new cultural paradigm should be based on a common-sense universal philosophy that transcends cultural and gender differences and is aimed at providing an equitable lifestyle with a sustainable economy that protects and preserves the Earth.

This new cultural paradigm must be based on a correct and clear knowledge of how people are programmed to think and behave the way they do—and that is the province of education, first by parents and then by teachers and the public media.

It goes without repeating that there are more than a dozen categories of thinking and behavior in the present-day American mindset that are seriously harmful to the mental and physical wellbeing of Americans—not to mention the image and the influence of the U.S. abroad. Among the flaws that are the most damaging:

1) Religious-based moralities that have not resulted in a moral peaceful society.

2) Male dominance in virtually all fields.

3) The new and insidious money morality.

4) The free speech provision in the Constitution that is misused and abused.

5) The money-driven legal morass that often makes a mockery of justice.

6) The excess consumption syndrome that now permeates the American economic system and is rapidly spreading around the world.

The failure of god-based moralities is a no-brainer. The original intent of the men who created the religions was to provide positive guidelines for their particular tribe or society. Given the volume and variety of "sin" in every human society that continues to occur the original plans obviously didn't work out.

Although not original, several of the 10 command-ments of Moses were on track but they were quickly de-based and/or ignored by most people, particularly those in power.

One of the worst elements in the Christian God myth, mentioned earlier, is that you can "sin" like hell until you are on your death-bed, and then all you have to do to get a free pass to Heaven is confess your sins and claim to believe that a historical figure now known as Jesus Christ is your savior. Again, that is the ultimate of all cop-outs.

It obviously goes without saying that to truly meet the physical, emotional, intellectual and spiritual needs of mankind the world needs a new, global, cultural para-digm—one that "fits" and enhances the lives of everybody in all societies. But are there principles and policies that would ensure high standards of ethical behavior and would work on a worldwide basis?

There are, but to create and implement this new para-digm would mean discarding all of the institutionalized and ritualized one-God cult religions. [The only difference between these three cults and notorious little cults is that these three are very big and very powerful, and can ignore and squash criticism.]

It is, of course, a fact that some of the social tenets of Judaism and Christianity are responsible for much of the humane morality that has managed to survive in the United

149

States and other Western countries. But even the most casual glance at the level of morality in so-called Christianized societies reveals that corruption and immoralities of all kinds are thriving as never before.

Of course, all branches of Christianity now present themselves as humane and nurturing. But all of them are still off-base in many of their teachings—and have never been and are not now capable of instilling a desirable standard of morality even in "Christianized" countries, much less universally.

In some respects the Islam that controls some countries is even worse. It remains in part caught in a time warp, with many of the same irrational and barbarous tenets that were the bedrock of Christianity for many centuries—the same Christianity that was responsible for the crusades against Muslims, for the Catholic Inquisitors who tortured and burned dozens of thousands over a period of several generations, for the depredations of the Spanish Conquistadors in the New World, for the European Colonialists and their campaigns to subjugate native populations in Africa and to eradicate them in North and South America, and on and on.

And there is another very conspicuous obstacle to the creation and implementation of a new code of ethics for humanity. This obstacle is a large number of professional people world-wide in think tanks, in universities, and in other organizations that have agendas that range from being anti-white, anti-black, anti-Jewish, anti-Islamic, anti-democratic, anti-capitalism, anti-globalism, anti-American, to anti-international business, and more.

As is also obvious, these groups now have the means to reach millions of people daily with their virulent messages. A recent book entitled *Welcome to the Ivory Tower of Babel* by Michael Adams presents a fascinating and frightening portrait of these think-tank and campus-based anti-everything groups.

Guidelines for a
New Cultural Paradigm

So what might a new social paradigm look like—one that all people could live by and achieve their fullest potential? Being as practical as possible, given what is known about humanity, the new cultural paradigm would have to include the following:

1] That all governments be based on the best principles of democracy.

2] That all societies acknowledge and follow the fundamental principle that females have an equal stake in humanity and must have the same rights and same opportunities as males.

3] That morality be based on dogma-free principles that recognize the true nature of mankind and are designed to nurture all of the elements in the make-up of human beings: the body, the emotions, the intellect and the spirit.

4] That the educational policies of all governments and all educational institutions be redesigned to inculcate all students from day one with a genteel standard of behavior; a moral value system that includes respect for others, honesty, truthfulness and diligence; a sense of pride in themselves; a sense of honor; the ambition to make the world a better place; and the courage to have big dreams.

5] That the economic policies of all governments be redesigned to further a global-based process of raising the living standards of all people on the planet to a comfortable level.

6] That the finite nature and fragility of Planet Earth be totally recognized and that universal mandatory directives be established to protect and sustain it… balanced with the profit-making that is essential for any business!

7] That these goals be made the basic charter of mankind and be pursued on a global, coordinated basis.

Of course, there are hundreds of other factors real and imagined that would have to be a part of this paradigm shift. What I am saying is that all societies on the planet must become inter-connected to the point that they are, in fact, members of a global society. A very old idea—a global village!

We've gone from a Cold War of political ideologies to a Hot War of religious ideologies. And that is the new reality of the 21st century. We must therefore strive with everything in our power to bring all countries into the same rational, logical, humane, human family.

And the United States, despite its many shortcomings, is the best hope for leading the world in a crusade for a sane, rational, comprehensive, universal morality. Much of the world is, in fact, waiting for us to create and demonstrate a morality that would lift mankind up and out of the religious, political and economic muck and mire of history.

We have very obviously already attempted to start this crusade. But we have failed to do enough of the educational groundwork necessary to bring the mass of humanity on board the effort, even in the United States!

I fault all of the Establishments for this failure: first the Religious Establishments, then the Political Establishments, followed by Business Establishments and most of all in more recent times the Educational Establishments.

The Education Establishment is the guiltiest of all in failing to provide a foundation for a truly humane and, ethical world society because the majority of educators know—or should know—what is myth and what is factual; what is good for humanity and what is not good!

But most of the people making up Educational Establishments worldwide, like many people in political institutions, are more self-serving than society-serving—not always by choice but because of the systems we've created. Furthermore, academia, like religion, attracts zealots whose goals serve their own agendas, not mankind. And again it goes without saying that one of the primary causes for the failure of education throughout history has been the baleful influence of religions.

Of course, there is a lot of complaining and wailing about these systems. But like religious and political institutions, educational organizations are too divided, too hemmed in by laws, too entrenched, and too bureaucratic to reform themselves.

Because public schools are financed by national governments and/or states, politicians are involved in virtually every aspect of education. Making education subject to the whims and wills of legislators has been said to be like turning the design of an elephant over to committees whose members have never seen one.

The decisions that lawmakers make impact directly on the actions of superintendents and teachers, requiring them to implement and enforce policies and practices that are often detrimental to the education process.

The only feasible answer to this dilemma is probably a panel made up of people who are not members of legislatures but are given the authority to make recommendations that are binding on them.

Saving the Earth from People!

One of the most important—and most vital—of the steps that must be taken to protect and preserve the Earth and its life forms is to make family planning universal and mandatory on a world-wide basis. That is a cultural challenge the likes of which most countries have never faced. But not meeting the challenge is too horrible to contemplate.

As recent as 1873 the male-dominated American Congress *passed a law labeling birth-control information obscene and banning its distribution to the public.*

China was apparently the first nation to implement a population control program. In 1979 supreme leader Deng Xiao-ping decreed that ethnic Han Chinese couples in urban areas of the country could not have more than one child in a desperate measure to stop the ballooning of the population that had already exceeded one billion.

Deng was able to make this draconian policy stick because he had absolute control of the country and did not face the wrath of religious zealots whose God demands that couples have as many children as is physically possible—a practice that traditionally has been more acceptable to men than to women.

In advanced and developing countries the reduction in population growth rate is well underway because wives in particular and a growing number of husbands made the decision on their own to limit the size of their families, regardless of their religious affiliations.

This movement is based on immediate economic factors as well as on a growing awareness that large families are not as desirable as they used to be. But broadly speaking it is far below what is necessary to lower the overall population of the Earth.

Still, it has been shown repeatedly that when wives in poverty-stricken countries are provided with the means to avoid multiple pregnancies many of them will do so—a very hopeful sign.

But reducing the overall birthrate much less achieving a negative birthrate will require a combination of government will on an international basis and a fundamental change in the position of religions that promote large families as "God's will." You cannot be more short-sighted!

In fact, the world needs some kind of parenting code of ethics that people be taught before they get married and

154

have children—in or outside of wedlock. To start with, courses in parenting responsibilities and skills should be made a mandatory part of the education of the young. But there must be more. There must be a universal family planning program that brings rationality and practicality into procreation.

One of the most critical factors in American society that makes the population problem even more pressing has been the preponderance of young single women, particular Blacks and Hispanics, who have children—something that developed because of sexually aggressive and irresponsible males responding to a macho culture and a government system of supporting single women who become parents.

And then to add to the problem, popular culture began before the turn of the century to subtlety condone unmarried women in all racial and culture backgrounds having children out of wedlock—a phenomenon that originated in the entertainment world.

The battle for women's right to control the number of children they have is far from over. Individual religious zealots in the private sector as well as many who are in public office are keeping the fight going by opposing family planning in any form or fashion—with many resorting to mental and physical intimidation, and some to murder.

As of this writing national polls show that over two-thirds of young American males and females believe that the ability to prevent unwanted pregnancies is important, but 63 percent say they know very little about birth control pills, and much of what they say they know is wrong.

All public institutions and organizations, including the religions, should join together to make the Pill available to females worldwide. Each Pill costs only a few cents to produce, and they could be made available for free-pickup in places in every city, town, village and rural area in the world.

But the responsibility of controlling the population of the Earth should not and will not be left up to females alone. As of 2010 dramatic advances had been made by American scientists in the development of new means of preventing conception for both women and men. Whether or not males make use of this new technology will be the ultimate test of their concern, both for their female partners and the Earth.

And unfortunately the people primarily responsible for approving and advocating that decision on the highest level are males who have irrational religious objections.

The Battle over the Pill

While the importance of having as many children as possible had some justification in earlier times when the population of the Earth was small, life-expectancy was short and dangerous diseases often caused mass extincttions.

Now, whether expressed or not, the motivation of some religions for unrestricted fertility among their members is primarily to increase their numbers and their financial and political power because they know that virtually all of their membership comes from members having more children who can be programmed in the dogma of the religion, not by proselytizing among adults.

In the past, the proselytizing success that Christianity and its offshoots have had has invariably been in poor countries where women were oppressed. These successes did not come from the theology or spirituality the missionaries preached but from the gender and social reforms they advocated. [Most missionaries ended up teaching English, and their only true "converts" were the children they taught.]

The mistreated and unhappy people in these countries should have learned long ago that believing in, bowing before, and praying to spirits and gods did not improve their political or social situation one iota. That is something that requires fundamental reforms in political and social institutions over which even "gods" have no control.

The religious-economic-political concept that prosperity and the quality of life is based on a continuously growing population is not only out-dated, it is one of the primary factors in the poverty that plagues over half of the population of the Earth, including millions of people in the most prosperous nations. Over-population is also one of the primary sources of much of the violence that afflicts so much of mankind.

The common sense of females, the power of technology and a growing number of enlightened males now offer mankind an opportunity to solve what is potentially one of the greatest problems human beings have ever faced—how to get population growth under control and create a new universal cultural paradigm.

Attempts to prevent pregnancy in females go back at least three thousand years [and included some far out methods], but nothing really worked well until the development of the Pill in 1950s by American scientists, and its approval by the Food and Drug Administration in 1960. At that time the typical American woman had 3.6 children.

Just one of these contraceptive pills a day was effective over 92 percent of the time in preventing pregnancy. Side effects were rare [and have since been virtually eliminated]. When first introduced each pill cost only 12 cents.

At that time, attempts to prevent pregnancy were banned by a number of religions and there were actually laws in various religions-oriented states and countries making family planning a criminal offense.

First, women by the thousands began taking the tiny pill daily, despite the laws and religious edicts, and their numbers continued to grow. By 1980 the birth rate among white Americans had dropped below two for the first time in the history of the country.

Despite the fact that the primitive bastions of male power kept up the battle year after year to prevent women from taking the Pill, their numbers soon passed a million, then ten million and by 2010 well over one hundred million.

The gradual unfolding of this pregnancy revolution by American women was chronicled by *TIME* magazine in 2010, recounting a battle that started several thousand years ago, and is still in its early stage.

Some of the methods used in an effort to prevent pregnancy in ancient times were bizarre to say the least—including such things as the male putting a ring made from a cut lemon around his penis.

Well into the 20th century contraception of any kind was opposed by orthodox religions around the world, the most powerful of which even regarded sex within marriage as immoral unless it was aimed at having children. Families with up to 14 or more children were widely praised and held up as paragons of moral behavior.

Women, including some Catholic women, who began to push for effective birth-control methods were treated as criminals. Margaret Sanger, one of the first major figures in this battle, took up the fight after her mother died from complications caused by 18 pregnancies.

She wrote that she dreamed of a "magic pill," and in 1916 she opened a birth-control clinic in Brooklyn, New York. The clinic was raided by the police, she was arrested and spent time in jail for her efforts.

Not surprisingly, the man who was ultimately responsible for the development of the Pill began his research in an effort to *increase fertility in women who were having trouble conceiving*—not blocking pregnancies!

The emancipation of American women from getting pregnant every 21 or 22 months was to have a profound influence on the social and economic situation of females, contributing to them swarming into universities and corporate offices by the millions.

By the end of the 20th century some lower level religious leaders had bowed to the inevitable and given grudging approval of the Pill for married women—or they kept quiet about it because they knew large numbers of their members had been using it for many years.

Still today there is tremendous opposition to the Pill by religious institutions in the U.S. and elsewhere by critics in some African countries who say it is being used as a political weapon by the White race to limit the number of Blacks. Some conservative politicians in the United States attempt to claim the moral high ground by opposing artificial means of contraception.

But as history has proven over and over again, nothing changes human behavior faster and more completely than new technology that makes life easier and better. Technology that has benefits that are immediately obvious changes physical behavior virtually instantly—*and a change in thinking inevitably follows.*

This phenomenon began ages ago but it did not come into its own until the 20th century, and it now drives humanity. The challenge is to curb the misuse of technology through education in all areas and levels of society—something that is not possible without an overall paradigm shift in the culture.

The Economic Growth Obsession

Another vital factor in saving the Earth is eliminating the political, economic and social policies of promoting economic growth and more growth for the sake of profit and power. Economic growth should first of all be designed to raise the level of the living standard of all people on Earth to a comfortable level that it is sustainable—and then economic policies should be based on improving the quality of life.

This is another area that must be addressed by not only by the education system but by the news media, the business world, the political establishments, and by ordinary people who understand that there must be a limit to economic growth.

The Gross National Product [GNP] of a nation should not be the standard by which it is measured. That is a mindset that inevitably leads to irrational and immoral behavior. It permeates a culture and leads to competition that in turn can and has led to war.

There are some societies that are not as obsessed with GNP as the United States, China, Japan and other industrialized nations. But to my knowledge as of this writing only tiny Bhutan in Southeast Asia has an official policy that promotes *Gross National Happiness* [GNH] instead of GNP. There were, however, a growing number of countries that were beginning to give more priority to GNH, including [not surprisingly] France, resulting in many foreigners beating up on the French for their "irrational" behavior.

The political, economic and social policies of promoting growth and more growth for the sake of growth and power must be eliminated from the human mindset. Economic growth should first of all be designed to raise the level of the living standard of all people on Earth to a comfortable level while ensuring that it is sustainable.

Transforming a society from an economic base to a happiness base is an educational challenge. It will not happen from the top down. It must be a personal choice made by individuals and families and grow from the bottom up.

It is also obvious that the material quality of life is primarily determined by knowing what to do and having the political and religious freedom to do it. This makes it imperative that all people be freed from the destructive religious, political and economic shackles of the past.

Understanding & Using
The Power of Language

The history of mankind proves that the world will never know universal peace and goodwill toward all until fundamental cultural differences, particularly religions, are resolved—or at least diminished to the point that they can be settled without resorting to war.

Despite all of the ranting and railing that it would cause, I propose that one of the fastest and most effective means of contributing to this goal would be for all non-English speaking people in the world to be required to learn English as a second language—something that is already occurring on its own, just too slowly.

This would not mean that people would have to give up their native languages or the facets of their culture that are positive and nurturing. But it could and would mean that the logical, rational cultural elements that are bound up in English would help make it possible for them to think and behave on the same wavelength—if they chose to do so.

As noted earlier, key words in languages are both the reservoir and transmitter of cultures. Learning any language well—that is to the point that you have absorbed its nuances and uses spiritually and physically as well as intellectually—adds the essence of that culture to your mindset.

Full understanding of a culture may be achieved intellectually from reading books, but only learning the language within the culture gives you emotional and spiritual understanding.

There are also key words in the English language that incorporate all of the values and traits that make up the truly ideal individual, and just learning these key words really well in all of their cultural meanings and uses can have a dramatic impact on the attitudes and behavior of an individual when they are reacting to and/or interacting with native English speakers...and among themselves.

The movement toward English becoming the international language is already well underway but at its present pace it could take fifty to a hundred or more years before it is wide-spread enough to significantly reduce misunderstandings and disagreements to a manageable level.

Promoting the teaching of English on a worldwide basis would be something that the United States, Great Britain, other English speaking nations, and the United Nations should be able to do—the latter after it overcomes resistance from its own delegates. It would be a lot less destructive, less wasteful and less costly than war.

The Importance of Physical Skills

One of the greatest failings of most middle and upper class families in America today is not understanding or ignoring the vital role that physical skills can play in the lives of both children and adults...and I am not talking about playing games or sports.

A skill as simple as juggling balls or other objects with the hands can have a positive and remarkable influence on one's life. It will attract favorable attention to you, open doors for you, and provide you with opportunities for interacting with people who can help you achieve your goals.

Many children today learn how to operate computers and other high-tech devices faster than their parents and other adults. But such learning should not be limited to such devices. It should also include things like using kitchen utensils, carpentry tools, repair tools, and so on—and parents that fail to teach such skills to their children or provide them with the opportunity to learn such skills are short-changing them.

Learning how to fix ordinary things around a house not only saves lots of money and inconvenience, it is also a source of self-confidence—not to mention the satisfaction it provides from being able to help yourself and others.

The Key to Mastering Anything

Artists and craftsmen learned ages ago that the key to mastering any art or craft is to first identify all of the steps in the process, categorize and label them, and then practice them in the proper order over and over until the process becomes imprinted not only on the mind but more importantly on the body.

The point of this repetition is to reach the point where you do not have to *think* about the process in order to accomplish it perfectly. The goal is to practice until it becomes an automatic function—a process used—but generally not verbalized in the West—by all people who master an art or skill of any kind.

Musicians, sports people, painters and many others must practice the individual steps of their art or craft over and over, and not just to reach the initial mastery. They must continue to practice often if not daily as long as they want or need to perform at the highest level of their profession.

This concept permeated the traditional cultures of China, Korea and Japan, and remains today a powerful factor in their economic success. With the exception of art, some sports and entertainment skills this concept is rare in contemporary American culture.

The Value of Cursive Writing

The status of cursive writing in the U.S. is yet another hole in the education system. By the first decade of the 21st century it was obvious that the level of cursive handwriting in the United States had degenerated to the point that many students could hardly write a legible sentence. Some could neither write nor read cursive handwriting. But very little if any action was taken by either parents or teachers to remedy the situation.

What parents and educators should be aware of and concerned about is that the benefits of learning cursive writing go well beyond a method of recording and communicating—which now, of course, can be done by one-finger or one-thumb typing.

Learning cursive writing well—to the point that it has some artistic value—teaches hand and eye coordination, diligence and perseverance—skills that are vitally important in virtually all other areas of life. It also instills pride in the individual and impresses other people.

What most Americans appear to be totally ignorant of— or could care less about—is the fact that the very complicated traditional writing system in China, Japan and Korea was a major contributing factor in their rise to economic and political prominence.

Instead of the simple 26 ABCs that make up English, Chinese, Japanese and Korean students must learn to read and write [actually *draw*!] from 2000 to 3000 ideograms in order to advance up the grades and graduate from high school. The ideograms, created in China some three to five thousand years ago [there are, in fact, a total of some 50,000 of them in ancient Chinese texts] and eventually adopted by Koreans and Japanese, consist of one to more than 20 strokes.

To be acceptable, the strokes of the ideograms—or characters as they are also called in English—must be made in a precise order. In many cases, parents start their children on learning how to draw *and paint* the characters when they are three or four years old. The process is continued and intensified in kindergarten and the first several years of grade school. They are the fundamental building blocks of all education in China, Japan and South Korea.

Unlike the Roman letters, every Chinese ideogram has a precise pictorial meaning of its own. In other words, it presents a picture of a concept...made up of one to more than two dozen elements. While English must be read or pronounced to have meaning, the meaning of Chinese characters is built in.

Learning to read and draw the minimum number of ideograms to get through high school in China, Japan and Korea requires years of dedicated, diligent study and practice that impacts directly on the mental attributes and physical skills of each new generation.

In earlier times in these countries the character and cultural accomplishments of individuals was measured by how well, how artistically, they could draw ideograms.

I recently came across an astonishing newspaper column written by Joanie Flatt, a public relations professional, who was decrying the fact that most young people in their teens and twenties could not read anything in cursive writing and had to have greeting cards and invitations they received written in cursive translated by an older adult.

She went on to quote a California English teacher who said that few of her students could write or read cursive, with this added startling comment: "But the kids I teach who *can* produce the most beautiful cursive are the family members of criminals—gang members who practiced gorgeous cursive in prison then passed it on to their sons and nephews when they get out."

That was an amazing indictment of the state of American culture today.

I am not suggesting that Americans adopt the Chinese ideographic system of writing, but I am saying that learning how to write the Roman alphabet in cursive letters has real, measureable value that impacts on the whole culture.

Learning to read and write cursive English with just 26 letters is child's play compared to what Chinese, Korean and Japanese children learn between the ages of 3 and 15—and it shows.

A Teacher Who Learned How to Teach!

Frustrated inner-city Chicago high school teacher Jack Canfield spent years trying to find ways to motivate his students to actually study and learn, finally discovering that the secret was as simple as instilling in them a positive attitude and high self-esteem.

After discovering this "amazing secret," Canfield began holding seminars to teach other teachers how to teach. He then began putting the lessons he had leaned into a series of "Chicken Soup for the Soul" books. Since 1993 he has edited and published well over 200 "Chicken Soup" titles and sold over 125 million copies in 47 languages.

Dealing with the Problem of Sex

Throughout history the 90 to 95 percent of all human beings who have desired only to live and let live and be safe and secure have not had the power to dispute or ignore their religious, political, and military rulers, all of whom have had their sexual do's and don'ts that added to rather than solved the problem of human sexuality.

As already noted, the blatant, gross use of sex in business is one of the most negative legacies of the religious distortion and repression of the sexual impulse. Even once straight-laced Asian countries have picked up on the American practice of using sex to sell. This misuse and abuse of human sexuality is also not going to go away until we manage to create a new ethic for sexual behavior that is rational, satisfying and doable.

Just one of thousands of daily examples of the inadequacies of the present system: in India official statistics estimate that there are some 1.2 million child prostitutes. The number of child prostitutes in African nations and in other nations as well, including the United States, is both staggering and astonishing.

There is no mystery at all as to why this incredible situation exists and has existed for millennia. In short, the sexual nature of the human male, male-dominated religions and male-dominated political, economic and social systems are responsible.

This situation will not be eradicated until enough men of goodwill find the courage and the voice to defy the misplaced moral teachings of religions and other anti-human ideologists to demand that the sexual nature of human beings be recognized and a rational, practical system for accommodating this nature be accepted as the norm.

Interestingly, as is almost always the case when it comes to cultural changes, it is and will be younger people, not leaders, who bring the final solution to the sex problem—and now with the entertainment and news industries pushing the process and the Internet providing them with instant access to billions of people that could happen within the 21st century.

When this happens the sex-based advertising, entertainment and news based industries as well as the anti-sex positions of religions will have to find something else to justify their existence. With the time span of each generation getting shorter and shorter, there may yet be foreseeable hope for humanity.

Closing the Black Hole of Summer

According to experts, one of the reasons for the failings of the American education system is the tradition of summer vacation. Experts agree that summer-long vacations for students have out-lived their usefulness, and are now a major weakness in the system.

Originally began to allow children to help with farming chores, long summer vacations now acts as "black holes," with many students forgetting much of what they learned during the previous semester. Published data has revealed that by the 9th grade summer learning loss could be blamed for roughly two-thirds of the achievement gap separating income groups. Problems caused by summer vacations were first documented in 1906 and they have increased every year since.

TIME Magazine's David Von Drehele writes: "It's an outdated legacy of the farm economy. But those months out of school do most damage to the kids who can least afford it."

Research by Duke University's learning expert Harris Cooper reveals that on average all students lose about a month of progress in math skills each summer, while low income students slip as many as three months in reading comprehension.

A research team at Johns Hopkins University examined more than 20 years of data tracking students from kindergarten through high school, found that regardless of the income levels better-off kids remembered most of what they had learn the previous semester while disadvantaged students fell back as much as three grades by the time they finished grammar school.

Education experts say that until summer vacations become a thing of the past parents should do everything possible to get their elementary and high school children into summer programs that combine fun and learning— something referred to as "stealth learning."

A full year of schooling with short vacations spread through-out the year over special national holidays is just plain common sense. But with more and more education being based on technology and available anywhere any time this problem may simply disappear.

A Willful Stupidity Checklist

Albert Einstein is on record as saying that there are two things that are infinite: the universe and human stupidity, and that he was not sure about the universe.

While it is true that in recent decades human beings have accomplished things that are god-like, we have not only continued to behave with willful stupidity, we have dramatically enlarged on the variety and volume of stupid things we do—knowing that they are harmful to people, to all other life forms and to the planet—all faults that can be blamed on parental, administrator and teacher failings.

The following things can be ranked among the most stupid and most damaging characteristics of humans—all of which impact on the motivation and ability of parents and teachers to educate the young.

1] The widespread existence of violence in every form imaginable, from mental and physical abuse to murder and war—most often committed by men.

2] Belief in male-created religious dogma that represses natural human behavior—especially our genetically programmed sexuality—and encourages discrimination and violence against non-believers—the latter invariably perpetrated by men.

3] The male-led adoption of the profit motive as the primary human morality, overriding all of the valid moral teachings of religions and philosophers.

4] The creation of huge entertainment industries based on appealing to unfulfilled sexual appetites that religions have traditionally sought to repress, thus creating the market.

5] The display of female sexuality as a come-on to attract attention to products and services because female sexuality has been denied, covered up, abused and limited by religion-based social customs and laws, creating an obsessive interest in it.

6] Built-in discrimination against different races, colors and religious creeds caused by ego-based self-interest, tribalism, territorialism and the thirst for power and control.

7] The glorification of the use of drugs by the entertainment industries and the concentrated efforts of the medicinal drug industry to get more people to take more drugs in a profit-making conspiracy with the medical field.

8] The breakdown of the male-female family unit as the primary structure of societies, and the growing number of males who impregnate single females and take no role in the upbringing of the children they sire.

9] The failure of more and more parents in industrialized countries to take responsibility for civilizing and educating their children, leaving it up to television, video games and "conveyor-belt" schools.

10] The reality that virtually all of the organized structures of modern society—business, education, government, health—are primarily based on self-interest within a mish-mash of guidelines and rules that are self-limiting if not self-defeating.

Virtually all of these failings are the result of willful stupidity, and that is not going to go away or be significantly reduced until we have a new universal cultural paradigm in place and working.

Teaching a Global Perspective

All education in the United States should have a global perspective, as represented by the program provided by International Baccalaureate [IB] which began in 1968 in

Switzerland and as of this writing has spread to more than 3,000 public schools in 139 countries.

The not-for-profit International Baccalaureate Organization depends upon government and private funding to train its teachers and implement its programs. Its goal is to foster curiosity, critical thinking skills and a global perspective—all critical attributes in today's world. One of the most popular elements of the BI system is its dual language program. A growing number of parents *want* their children to be at least bilingual.

Students who want to pursue their career choice in college should naturally be encouraged to major in those subjects that are related to their life goals, including the study of and the experiencing of foreign cultures and languages.

Japanese companies re-initiated this foreign culture and foreign language program for new employees in the 1950s [they originally initiated it in the late 1870s when Japan was in the throes of industrialization after the fall of the Shogunate and clan system of government in 1867]. South Korean companies followed the Japanese example in the 1960s. The Chinese government made foreign language and foreign culture programs a national priority for college students in 1990s. India also joined in before the end of the 20th century.

Our European competitors have had the advantage of large numbers of their people being at least bilingual if not multi-lingual and multi-cultural since the late 1800s. And Americans wonder why the U.S. has so many problems with its foreign political and business affairs!

The reason, in part, is simple: the failure of our political, business and education leaders to create an education system that has a global perspective and makes global sense.

Technology as God!

Given all the negative influences in today's cultures, the only salvation for humanity may be the positive influence of technology—which by itself is already rapidly changing all of the world's cultures. In the long run, even without courageous forward-thinking and forward-acting leaders, the world's cultures will become more and more rational, and more and more democratic because of the income-parable ability of technology to inform, to educate, to encourage critical thinking and to change the behavior of people—and especially to influence people to demand their natural rights to be free and have choices.

But given the fact that primitive religions and authoritarian political forms still have a death-grip on most of mankind these transformations could take generations—time the Earth does not have—because leaders will not or cannot take the heroic steps necessary to change today's morality and today's policies even if they *want* these things to happen!

And, of course, there are regional and national leaders who are dead-set against such freedom and against a humane morality for the people they rule. As a result, many people may continue to be oppressed and prevented from achieving their full potential for generations to come unless these changes are aggressively promoted by huge numbers of people blogging the world's bureaucrats and leaders in business, in politics and in religions with criticism and advice, and even more importantly, by simply refusing to go along with stupid, insane policies and by voting the people who promote them out of office—or ignoring them if they cannot be removed from positions of power!

Of course, the majority of people everywhere are sickened by all of these cultural failures. But survival, power and profit-making—not moral behavior—are the overwhelming goals of most leaders in politics and business.

And as already said, there is no way that the weak, divided and often irrational god-based moralities of today are going to change that!

We therefore need to teach and follow a philosophy of living and working that is based on common sense, on the fragile nature of the Earth, on the real physical, emotional, intellectual, spiritual and philosophical needs of human beings.

There are millions of people already espousing these philosophies but with so little impact that contemplating the future is frightening.

Despite the misuse and abuse of the Internet by hate mongers, pornographers and radical religious zealots—not to mention people who are simply ignorant—this new technology also makes it possible for the average person to make his or her voice heard on a large scale for the first time in the history of mankind.

Ordinary people can now vote and express themselves online at any time on very important issues of the day! If enough rational, educated, morally enlightened people will bring more and more pressure against leaders in every field to force them to give up their self-serving ways—or force them out of positions of authority and let a new breed of people have a go at it—the ancient religious promise of peace on earth might be achieved.

Many Americans believe that freedom of religion, freedom of the press, freedom of assembly, and freedom of speech referred to in the First Amendment of the Constitution are constitutional rights...and that freedom of speech gives people the right to say or write almost anything, no matter how gross or harmful it might be.

It goes without saying that the Freedom of Speech provision in the First Amendments of the American Constitution should somehow be amended to prohibit its abuse by the so-called entertainment industries and others who

173

abuse it for profit and power, without reducing the basic intent of the provision.

In addition to being morally inexcusable, the present extreme interpretations and use of the Freedom of Speech provision are socially insane.

The hold that the new money morality has on the minds of most people will not change until technology has reached the point that the creation of products and services can be automated and made virtually free to consumers, at which point money and profit-making will no longer be needed.

In the meantime, there are measures that can be taken to fundamentally change the behavior of people—measures that are based on the realities of life, not abstract religious teachings.

The Coming God Syndrome

On the human-beings-as-god front, well before the end of the first half of this century people will be able to get their DNA sequenced for a small fee, if not free, and will have a map of what it means to be human and what the future may hold for them health and longevity wise. Sequencing the genomes of all common life forms will be routine, providing road maps for altering and or improving them.

The sequencing of the genomes of all diseases will have been accomplished, making it possible to eliminate them. The sequencing of matter is already well underway and is resulting in new materials never before seen or even imagined that will impact life on virtually every level.

Advances in all areas of science are becoming a daily thing; advances that will continue to transform what people do and how they do it.

The day of man as the real god-creator is at hand, but the question remains: can mankind ever be a benevolent god?

Learning Lessons from
Japan's Famous Samurai Class

The samurai were a special class of people who ruled Japan from 1192 until 1868—a total of 676 years during which the famous shoguns and their samurai warriors directed all of the affairs of the country.

Over the first four centuries of this long reign the samurai class, which became hereditary, developed a philosophy and a code of conduct that was to make them one of the most remarkable groups of people the world had ever seen. They brought a system of refined etiquette and strict ethics to their own lives, and ultimately to the lives of the common people of Japan, that has seldom been approached and never surpassed by any other society.

But the unique culture that the Japanese samurai created functioned extraordinarily well only because Japan was virtually isolated from the rest of the world and maintained strict barriers against outside influences. When this isolation from the rest of the world ended the reign of the samurai begin to self-destruct.

In the late 1860s, just 15 years after the United States sent a fleet of warships to Japan to demand that the country open its doors to diplomatic and trade relations with the rest of the world, the Shogunate system of government fell, and in 1870 the samurai class was officially abolished.

But it was progressive samurai from outlying fiefs who brought the downfall of the then feeble backward looking Shogunate government in Edo. It was the same progressive samurai who formed Japan's new government between 1868 and 1870, and it was ex-samurai who took the lead in industrializing and modernizing the country between 1870 and 1895—an astounding accomplishment that was made possible by the spirit, the character, the thirst for knowledge, the skills, and the unbounded ambition of former samurai.

By that momentous time in Japanese history, the positive principles of the samurai ethic had seeped into the culture of the common people, adding to their traditional honesty, diligence, loyalty, courage in the face of dangers, and their unquenchable spirit in the face of great challenges.

Unfortunately, when the new democratic Japan came face-to-face with the colonial policies of the Western powers the Japanese military gained the upper hand in the government and using both the good and bad elements of the culture that the samurai had created they set out to build their own colonial empire by attacking their neighbors and eventually the United States—and event that was predicted in 1915 by a Japanese sociologist.

Follow their defeat in this costly enterprise the Japanese turned their samurai-created traits into performing an economic miracle. From 1950 to 1970 they not only recovered from the devastation of that destructive war, *they turned Japan into the second largest economy in the world!*

As early as 1960, Japanese manufacturers and exporters were flooding the world's markets with high quality and innovative products. In addition, they were investing billions of dollars a year in foreign countries—particularly the United States—buying up real estate and trophy properties at such a pace and in such volume it seemed as if they would soon own the world.

Western business and political leaders had not yet become aware of the economic threat posed by the Japanese and did not take them seriously. It was not until the early 1970s that Westerners were stunned from their head-in-the-mud complacency by the inroads being made worldwide by the Japanese.

There were, of course, many external factors involved in this amazing transformation. But it was primarily the character and the spirit that the Japanese had inherited from the samurai culture, combined with the physical skills that were created and sustained by the culture that made this astounding feat possible.

The principles and practices that made up the samurai way are just as valid today as they were during the long Shogunate period in Japan's history. In fact, most of them are common sense things raised to a much higher level than has been common in the rest of the world.

Of equal importance, these principles and practices were not separate from the common culture. They were an integral part of it. Individuals learned and lived the Japanese way from infancy.

This learning process was physical, intellectual and spiritual. The process of absorbing Japanese etiquette began in infancy. Infants and toddlers naturally learned and imitated the manners of their parents and others. In addition, they were endlessly subjected to both physical and verbal direction in manners and behavior in general.

Mothers and others constantly trained the very young in how and when to bow, in how to sit, how to eat—how to do all of the things that made up the Japanese way.

One of the most important elements in the training of all young Japanese, both indirectly and directly, was in the choice of vocabulary and in the manner of speaking.

Another key element in the programming of all Japanese was in respect—respecting the fragility of Japanese homes; respecting their parents, their elders, their teachers, the authorities, and so on.

Another factor in the training of young Japanese that was to set them apart was unbounded appreciation for the beauty of nature and for the materials and designs of their arts and crafts.

As already mentioned, the role that the Japanese writing system—the famous *Kanji* (kahn-jee) or ideograms imported from China—played in fashioning the character and abilities of the Japanese was another fundamental element in Japanese culture that was promoted and sustained by the samurai class.

The positive attributes that learning and using *Kanji* contributed to the mental makeup and physical skills of the Japanese is still not fully appreciated. Instead of having to learn just 26 letters, to be literate early Japanese had to learn to read and draw over 3,000 characters, some with as many as 25 strokes that had to be done in the right order! The number of *Kanji* present-day Japanese students must learn has been reduced to 1,945.

The training of the samurai during Japan's long feudal era got down to the basics of the mental and physical skills they needed to succeed in life because it was what they had to master to stay alive from one day to the next.

In the samurai philosophy, self-interest is one of the greatest faults because it skewers both thinking and behavior. Young samurai youths were taught that those who primarily think only of themselves and what pleases or benefits them cannot become true samurai.

One of the primary rules of the samurai was the importance of seeking out and learning from others who are smarter and more skilled than you are. Not everyone has the same IQ, but virtually everyone is capable of benefiting from the advice and counseling of people who are more experienced and more knowledgeable.

The samurai had also learned long ago that the intelligence of many is often superior to the intelligence of one, and that for many "consulting with people of good sense" is the ideal way of expanding one's store of knowledge, skills and chances for success in life.

This advantage, the samurai added, is not limited to you improving your abilities. Others, seeing that you are intelligent enough and ambitious enough to consult with people who are more experienced and wiser, will treat you with more than ordinary respect and go out of their way to help and support you.

Loyalty to one's family, friends, classmates, co-workers and teachers was one of the foundations of the samurai code. The samurai understood that without loyalty one could not live with any sense of security or well-being, and that fear and suspicion—like alien viruses—would eat away at their confidence and trust.

Another of the teachings of the samurai that is especially applicable today is that it is not wise to express a strong opinion to someone who is not willing to listen to and sincerely consider the opinion. Such an approach only increases ill-will and the possibility of friction and possible violence.

The samurai way advises that one should first develop a close, personal relationship with the individuals concerned so that they will trust you and will listen to you with respect—even if they ultimately do not accept your position.

Another of the principles of the samurai was to never shame a person. How, they asked, can you expect to make people better by shaming them? This not only creates resentment, it closes the people's minds to further willing cooperation.

In their recognition of the realities of life, the samurai approach was to allow ordinary people a little bit of leeway in abiding by both custom and laws to prevent them from becoming frustrated, resentful and less cooperative in things that really mattered.

It was also the understanding of the samurai that people of ordinary intelligence, as well as those with lower than average intelligence, are often more trustworthy, more diligent, and more worthy than those of above average intelligence.

This bit of wisdom is obvious in virtually all well-functioning and peaceful societies. Recognizing this, it was common during Japan's long samurai period for provincial lords and others in power to seek the advice of ordinary people whose lives were distinguished by their selfless natures and no thought of gain for themselves.

Another principle of the samurai was to consciously work diligently and without end to make themselves better that day than they were the day before. Over the centuries, this philosophy became deeply embedded in Japanese culture, permeating the mindset and behavior of the people from an early age—and is the origin of the now famous *kaizen* [kigh-zen] or "continuous improvement" concept in Japanese industry.

One of the most important codes in the conduct of the samurai was to treat small things seriously and great things lightly. This philosophy was based on a keen understanding of the nature of human beings to generally behave the opposite way—treating big things seriously and small things lightly, if at all.

The samurai understood that people would naturally do their best to cope with big things—sometimes going too far—while letting little things go could eventually have disastrous affects, like a tiny hole in a dam that gradually enlarges and brings the dam down.

In its samurai context, this principle included everything one said and did during the course of a day, from personal grooming, cleaning up one's room, house and surroundings, to preparing for study, play, or work.

Where great things that are likely to occur were concerned, the samurai taught that one should think about them in advance, plan for any situation that might occur, and when the time comes handle them as routine affairs.

It is, of course, well-known that making mistakes can be a powerful teacher, increasing both the level of one's knowledge and skills. But in the world of the samurai a single mistake that was often very minor in the overall context of things could mean their death within seconds.

This provided the samurai with extraordinary motivation to hone their knowledge and skills to an equally extraordinary degree—not only their skill with the sword and other martial weapons, but also in their manners, their personal grooming, and keeping their things in order.

At the same time, the samurai understood that people who are so cautious they never make a mistake are often less diligent, less courageous, less loyal, less dependable and less likely to do outstanding things than those who take chances.

The samurai recognized that negligence—failure to do things that are right or that should be done—was a common human characteristic, and that it is necessary not only to be conscious of this failure at all times, but to extend every possible effort to overcome it.

The samurai code called upon them to consciously start each day with the firm determination that they would not be negligent during the day at any time about anything.

The samurai code held that being smart and skillful was not enough. One also had to have the determination to use this wisdom and skill in doing the right thing at the right time.

In the philosophy of the samurai those who seek to accumulate material things are making a serious mistake because excess things do not bring true happiness. Instead, they add to one's obligations and worries, and take up time that should be utilized in ways that will truly enhance the tranquility and quality of life.

It was the responsibility of all Japanese parents to begin the process of educating their children by providing them with the example and the guidance that is essential to putting them on the path to respectful, responsible, successful adulthood.

The Making of a Samurai

Here are the key concepts that made up the training of Samurai youth, which began when they were six or seven years old, and culminated when they were 15 and thereafter were regarded as adults with all of the heavy responsibilities this included.

Learning Refined Manners
Learning the Lesson of Human Kindness
Learning to Take Responsibility
Learning the Importance of Honesty
Learning to Appreciate Things
Learning the Importance of Compassion
Learning to be Well-Groomed at All Times
Learning to Keep Things in Order
Learning to Pay Respect to Others
Learning the Lesson of Setting Goals
Learning the Lesson of Discipline
Learning the Lesson of Perseverance
Learning the Lesson of Diligence
Learning the Lesson of Concentration
Learning How to Sharpen Your Mind
Learning the Power of Repetition
Learning the Lesson of Awareness
Learning the Lesson of Observing
Learning How to Clear the Mind
Learning to Understand Human Nature
Learning to Use Intuitive Intelligence
Learning to Use Emotional Intelligence
Learning to Use Cosmic Wisdom
Learning to Use the Power of "The Cosmic Force"
Learning the Importance of Harmony
Learning the Importance of Tranquility*

*Abridged from my book, *Samurai Principles & Practices that will Help Preteens & Teens in School, Sports, Social Activities & Choosing Careers.*

The Extraordinary
Benefits of Modern-Day Karate

There is another element in modern Japanese culture that is already making a difference in the character and the lives of hundreds of thousands of pre-teens, teens and adults around the globe, and that is a modernized version of one of Japan's most famous martial arts.

As simplistic, and perhaps as other-worldly as it may sound, there is one training program that all children could be enrolled in at an early age that would go a long way toward instilling in them the cultural attributes that are the most desirable and admirable in human beings—and the only thing their parents would have to do is enroll them in this program and keep them in it from around the age of five to fifteen or sixteen.

This program is nothing more than the physical, emotional, intellectual and philosophical training provided by the modern-day version of *karate* (kah-rah-tay).

Karate literally means "empty hand," and was first developed in China by Buddhist priests who needed a way to protect themselves from ruffians and brigands as they traveled about the country because they were prohibited from carrying weapons. It made its way to Japan through the kingdom of Okinawa, which had regular trade and cultural relations with China.

When the Okinawan kingdom was attacked by a Japanese war lord, whose fief was on the southern end of Kyushu, the lord's samurai warriors soon discovered that Okinawan males who were proficient in karate were formidable fighters in hand-to-hand combat. But karate was no match for the weapons and skills of the samurai who soon defeated the Okinawans and then co-opted the ancient Chinese martial art into their own training.

During the early decades of the Tokugawa era [1603-1867] karate was gradually subsumed into the training of all of the samurai who ruled Japan, and later became a part of the training of Japan's imperial army and police forces.

After the fall of the Tokugawa Shogunate in 1867 and dissolution of the samurai class in 1870 karate was transformed into a sport aimed at developing the character of the individual, with special emphasis on respect for others, concentration, self-confidence, diligence, a sense of order, perseverance, honesty, courage and compassion.

But once again the aims of karate were subverted by militarists in the early 1900s, and it was not until the early 1950s, after the end of World War II in 1945, that the character-building version of karate was reinstated.

Today most people around the world are familiar with the word karate as a result of movies, video games and comic books, and they tend to see it as a fighting technique. But it is no longer aimed at developing prowess in combat. It is aimed at building the kind of character and behavior that all parents would like to see in their children.

The popularity of training in modern karate is, in fact, growing in training centers around the world as more parents come to understand that its remarkable benefits include improving the character, personality and behavior of their children. As of this writing there are over 3,000 karate training centers in the U.S. alone.

The Benefits of Karate

The World of Martial Arts Information Center lists the following benefits of karate as: learning the value of time, the importance of perseverance in achieving success, the dignity of simplicity, the value of character, the power of kindness, the influence of example, the obligation of duty, the wisdom of economy, the virtue of patience, the improvement of talents and the importance of respect.

The extraordinary benefits of modern-day karate could and should be incorporated into the world's education systems.

There is, in fact, no way that an individual can get full control of his or her mind without the kind of training provided by karate, and for the best results this training should begin when he or she is very young—meaning, of course, that it has to be initiated and managed by a parent or some other adult, generally over a period of at least 10 years.

The more precise the forms that make up a training program and the more intensive the training program the more control that is developed over the mind and body. Karate training combines and harmonizes these physical and mental requirements.

As said, modern-day karate is designed to instill the most desirable and admirable character traits in those who practice the art. These traits include determination, diligence, perseverance, courage, respect for others, respect for one's self, a refined sense of right and wrong, and justice.

Karate is not the final word in training children and teenagers but it is far superior to any other training method that is available for young and old alike. In addition to addressing the physical and mental side of one's being it also provides a philosophical base that is essential for a fully balanced life.

I believe the physical, intellectual and philosophical discipline provided by karate training could go a long way toward reducing many of the behavioral problems now plaguing American schools, and believe that karate should be made a permanent part of the education of the young, starting with K-2 or K-3 and continuing through K-12.

In the meantime, I suggest that you enroll your preteens and teens in karate classes at a nearby karate *dōjō* [dohh-johh].

Getting Control of the Spirit

The third most critical factor in the make-up of human beings is the spiritual element...and this does not refer to a belief in some religious dogma, which is often so far removed from reality that it is both ludicrous and anti-human.

Still today, despite millennia of learning and the development of an enormous reservoir of wisdom by many cultures, irrational religious beliefs continue to influence people to discriminate against, torture and kill each other in numbers that are incredible.

It now seems clear that the solution to this astounding human weakness will not be found in any organized religion, but in personal actions taken by individuals, including the nurturing and strengthening of the spirit.

This effort does not entail anything supernatural, divine or religious in any sense. It refers to all of the mental attributes that make up one's character and personality, and is a manifestation of the "force" that brings life to the body and mind. This spirit or life-force is something like a battery that runs our bodily functions, our thinking and most of our physical actions.

The power of this life-force, which various greatly in individuals, can be increased by physical exercises that challenge both the body and the mind. It can also be increased by learning how to focus the mind on a single thing—or emptying the mind altogether.

When the "spirit battery" is fully charged it includes such elements as courage, determination, diligence regarding both large and small things, perseverance in pursuing goals, an appreciation for form and order, harmonious personal relationships, and respect for all things.

As said, one of the primary goals of the modernized form of karate is to develop all of these elements by a type of training that is based on these factors. It introduces these elements to novice students as an integral part of the physical and mental training they undergo—not as abstract principles of behavior.

Karate students learn the lessons of how to think and behave in an ideal manner by actually performing the functions of the desired behavior...not by wrestling with abstract thoughts.

In this way, the philosophical aspects of karate are integrated into the body and the mind in a physical and mechanical sense. They become a part of the body and the mind.

Wise men and women learned a long time ago that when good behavior and knowledge are taught as physical subjects, not just as mental exercises, they become embedded in the body and mind and have a lasting effect.

"Body memory," as all great athletes, artists and performers know, is far more powerful and important than mental memory. Imagine master piano players having to consciously remember the locations of all of the keys they have to hit and consciously direct their fingers to those keys.

Both attitudes and social behavior can be instilled into the mind-body of the individual to the point that they become automatic.

Training the Intellect

Once children have achieved control of their body, mind and spirit though karate or any other method, the next step in becoming a fully civilized individual is to take full control of the intellect—the higher order of the mind that understands things, that makes choices and decisions based on rational, logical thinking and whatever experience and knowledge they have accumulated.

The final control of the intellect comes under the heading of philosophy, which refers to the love and pursuit of wisdom through intellectual means and moral self-discipline, with moral self-discipline being the key factor. Unfortunately, American educators have traditionally viewed philosophy as the province of eggheads who just sit around and think; not as one of the most essential elements of civilization and daily life.

Without rational and humane moral self-discipline there is no dependable compass or overriding guidelines for behavior, which is the reason why so many well-educated and experienced people do such terrible things.

It is obvious, of course, that present-day child-raising and educational systems in the U.S. and elsewhere do not get passing grades in either of these two areas. Again, the claim is not that long-term training in karate is the complete or final answer to these problems, but there is substantial evidence that it makes a remarkable difference in the character and personality of both boys and girls as well as adults of all ages.

The Distant Dream

All of the prevailing reasons why men go to war—religion, the hunger for political power, the obsession with wealth, territorial ambitions, oppressive government regimes—should be eliminated by a coordinated universal effort that now seems to be so far beyond the ability of mankind that it is not even a dream. But that is exactly what at least 95 percent of the people on Earth want! So why can't it be done?

It *can* be done but it will not be done until religious and political leaders are no longer in the dark ages where ignorance, irrationality and inhuman behavior are the norm—the norm for them; not for the people at large—or until new more powerful forces transform the mindset of humanity...a phenomenon that is already underway.

One of the most positive factors that has already raised the living standards of people in China and India—two countries that represent some two-thirds of humanity—was

188

work and production outsourced from the United States, Japan, South Korea and other developed countries.

As controversial and as painful to some as this phenomenon was, it nevertheless was the most efficient and practical means of achieving economic parity between nations—not tearing any of them down, but building all of them up.

The more affluent China, India and other developing countries became, the more they contributed to the economy of the countries outsourcing to them, the more stable their governments, and the more likely the leaders were to cherish and work for peace and prosperity.

Of course, there are many other things that should be done. And despite all of the gloom and doom scenarios I've harped on the great majority of people on this endangered planet are good-hearted, well-behaved and hardworking, and, again, want only to live peaceful, comfortable, secure lives.

The truly evil doers—leaders and their henchmen who are actually well-known to the world—number only in the few hundred thousand. If the world could somehow get rid of them and prevent others from taking their place the Earth could and surely would become a sane, safe habitat for humanity in a very short period of time.

It is obvious that the material quality of life is primarily determined by knowing what to do and having the political and religious freedom to do it. This makes it imperative that all people be freed from the destructive religious, political and economic shackles of the past.

It is also imperative that the excess-consumption syndrome be eliminated from the world's economic systems, and that people be encouraged and helped to create lifestyles that are physically, emotionally, spiritually and intellectually satisfying that are not based on excess material things.

Ordinary Americans have to become revolutionaries, willing to resist and to fight the status quo, and force all of the established power centers to do what is common sense and morally right for humanity and the Earth.

But still the Earth needs great leaders who are selfless and unrelenting in their efforts to protect and preserve the planet and mankind. As the great Chinese sage Lao Tzu said ages ago: "A great leader has no self-interest and leaves no trace. When he is finished the people say, 'We did it ourselves.'"

Lao also said that the more laws you have the more laws will be broken; and "When taxes are too high, people go hungry. When the government is too intrusive, people lose their spirit."

Interestingly, Mao Tse-Tung, the founder of the Chinese People's Republic in 1949, did virtually everything in his power to eliminate all influence and knowledge of China's greatest sages, Confucius and Lao Tzu, but his efforts were in vain. There was a renaissance of interest in both Confucianism and the teachings of Lao Tzu during the first decade of the 21st century, with both top political and military leaders publicly endorsing the wisdom of these ancient sages.

The New Education Paradigm

By the end of the first decade of the 21st century it was already obvious that technology was reshaping the model of education; that little by little teaching in most categories was transitioning into facilitating the use of technology— much of it in the hands of students themselves.

This is already having a fundamental impact not only on how students learn but what they learn because they are no longer chained to the institutionalized and ritualized methods and sources of learning. The future of both old, traditional teaching materials and teaching styles will be short, and this could be one of the fastest cultural transitions in the history of mankind.

This transition in teaching and learning can help lead to the reforming of all elements of American culture if it is allowed and encouraged to continue.

#

OTHER BOOKS BY THE AUTHOR

[Books on China]
The Chinese Mind—Understanding Traditional Chinese Beliefs and their Influence on Contemporary Culture
Chinese Etiquette & Ethics in Business
China's Cultural Code Words [Key Chinese Terms that Reveal the Culture and Mindset of the Chinese]
Chinese in Plain English
Survival Chinese / Instant Chinese
Etiquette Guide to China—Know the Rules that Make the Difference

[Books on Japan]
Japanese Etiquette & Ethics in Business
KATA—The Key to Understanding & Dealing with the Japanese
Japan's Cultural Code Words
Exotic Japan—The Sensual & Visual Pleasures
Discovering Cultural Japan
Speak Japanese Today—A Little Language Goes a Long Way!
Instant Japanese / Survival Japanese
Japan Made Easy—All You Need to Know to Enjoy Japan
Etiquette Guide to Japan—Know the Rules that Make the Difference
The Japanese Samurai Code—Classic Strategies for Success
Japan Unmasked—The Character & Culture of the Japanese
Elements of Japanese Design —Understanding & Using Japan's Classic *Wabi-Sabi-Shibui* Concepts
Samurai Strategies—42 Secret Martial Arts from Musashi's "Book of Five Rings"

191

Why the Japanese are a Superior People—The Advantages of Using Both Sides of Your Brain!
Amazing Japan—Why Japan is one of the World's Most Intriguing Countries
Exotic Japan—The Sensual & Visual Pleasures
SABURO—The Saga of a Teenage Samurai in 17th Century Japan
ONLY IN JAPAN!—The Bizarre & the Wondrous from the Land of the Rising Sun!

[Books on Korea]
Korean Business Etiquette
Korean in Plain English
Korea's Business & Cultural Code Words
Etiquette Guide to Korea— Know the Rules that Make the Difference
Instant Korean / Survival Korean

[Books on Mexico]
Why Mexicans Think & Behave the Way They Do—
The Cultural Factors that Created the Character & Personality of the Mexican People
Mexican Cultural Code Words [hard-cover]
There's a Word for It in Mexico [paperback]
Romantic Mexico—The Image & the Realities

[Other Titles]
Which Side of Your Brain Am I Talking To? – The Advantages of Using Both Sides of Your Brain
Samurai Principles & Practices that will Help Preteens & Teens in School, Sports, Social Activities & Choosing Careers
Romantic Hawaii—Sun, Sand, Surf & Sex
Asian Face Reading—Unlock the Secrets Hidden in the Human Face
Bridging Cultural Barriers in China, Japan, Korea & Mexico
EROS' REVENGE—Brave New World of American Sex!
THE ORIGINS OF HUMAN VIOLENCE! –
Male Dominance, Ignorance, Religions & Willful Stupidity!
ONCE A FOOL – From Japan to Alaska by Amphibious Jeep!

192